D0326714

*...for Sandra*

# Foreword

A lot has happened since the first edition of *Hiking Whatcom County* hit the shelves in 1987. While the total mileage of trails in the county still has not increased much, serious efforts are underway to develop trails and acquire public greenways and shoreline access in several communities. In 1990, for example, Bellingham voters approved a multi-million dollar levy to acquire trails and open space in what's become a nationally recognized urban greenway system. A similar county-wide measure has been discussed, but more people need to speak up to make it happen. On the plus side a master plan was completed in 1996 for Chuckanut Mountain trails. Lynden, Blaine, Everson, and Birch Bay have all shown strong support for trails and are beginning to see improvements on the ground.

The County adopted a Comprehensive Parks and Recreation Open Space Plan in 1989 that, if implemented, would substantially expand the county trail system, providing many loops and linkages, while interconnecting smaller communities, the Bellingham area trail network, and all major parks in the county. Hikers, equestrians and bicyclists participated in the plan. A random household survey was conducted in which *over 50% of county residents said they use trails and support the acquisition of more trails, parks and shoreline areas, even if it means raising taxes or restricting development.*

The Forest Service has shown more interest in trails and recreation in the Mt. Baker-Snoqualmie National Forest in recent years, thanks in part to public concern over old-growth forests and spotted owls. New trails and reconstruction projects are complete or underway in the Mt. Baker area, including Heather Meadows and the Wild Goose, East Bank Baker Lake, Scott Paul, Ridley Creek,

Elbow Lake, and Noisy Creek Trails. Budget cuts have put nearly all other projects on hold (cards and letters to Congress).

Countywide, the best trail projects stirring up interest today include the proposed 74-mile Bay-To-Baker Trail from Little Squalicum Beach to Shuksan Arm. The Chuckanut Mountain trail system (*see map on p. 140*) may link south Bellingham to Larrabee Park, Lost Lake, Chuckanut Ridge, Pine and Cedar Lakes, Lake Samish, Lizard and Lily Lakes, and Oyster Dome. Routes from Lake Whatcom to Bellingham Bay, connecting with Maritime Heritage Park and the planned Little Squalicum Park, are high on the city's list. Another would connect Lake Whatcom with Lookout Mountain and Lake Padden. There is also great potential for the south half of Lummi Island, the Smith Creek/Stewart Mountain area, Birch Bay, the north end of Sumas Mountain, Dewey Valley (a key section of the Bay-To-Baker Trail), and along the entire Nooksack River from Marietta to Maple Falls. Future trails along the South Fork Nooksack River and the Middle Fork gorge above Mosquito Lake Road bridge have excellent potential as well.

To achieve these lofty goals, a major funding initiative is needed to raise a million or two dollars by the year 2000 that, matched with grants, can be applied toward the purchase of critical corridors and easements (while they are available and affordable). With these and other resources, including volunteer efforts, we can begin to develop and maintain a respectable system of trails and bikeways. All the natural amenities, public support, and great ideas already exist.

Changing the subject, I want to emphasize that this guide is *not* intended to invite mountain bikes into all the areas described. As a rule, bikes are best suited to old road grades or more durable trails designated for such use (there are hundreds, if not thousands, of miles of unpaved roads in the region). On trails designed for feet, bikes can be obnoxious: they tear up the vegetation, replace smooth firm trail with ruts and mud holes, and they can be a hazard to other trail users. Despite the author's haranguing, mountain biking is a legitimate activity (I ride one myself), but not when it's to the detriment of the trail and those who tread more softly upon it...

On a more philosophical note (there is hidden meaning between these covers), there is something inherently nice about walking on trails. I don't know what it is, but it seems to have something to do with trees, rocks, birds, bugs, slugs, fresh air and streams that babble on forever. It's not the same as driving a car. It slows us down, wonderfully, and keeps us young and smiling. In fact, I have never encountered an unfriendly or unhappy camper on the trail, perhaps with the exception of an occasional cranky kid. If only we could encourage everyone to experience trails and wilderness... (hey, not all at once).

At last, some say a new environmental ethic is emerging, that people care more about this remarkable blue planet. We don't want to give up our cars or our habits of excess consumption, but at least we care (ditto heads and anti-enviro fanatics notwithstanding). If true, this new ethic, a positive long-term shift in fundamental societal values, may help us zero in on the harder personal and community choices still waiting to be made. On the trail, the choices we make ring clear. On the trail, "worries drop off like leaves" someone once said. Time slows down. Reality stares us down and we begin to get our priorities straight, whatever they may be... Well, hiking is also just plain fun. I hope this book is useful in that regard.

Many individuals offered advice, assistance and support which helped make this book a reality. Special thanks to Sara, Steve, all my hiking buddies, to Chuck, Dee and friends at Village Books, and to everyone on and off the trail who offered suggestions and encouragement to get it done.

Happy trails,

Ken Wilcox
Summer, 1996

# CONTENTS

**Walks & Hikes**   👣 = Easiest / 👣 👣 👣 👣 = Most Difficult

**The Coast**

**Urban & Lowland Trails**

**MT. BAKER AREA**          🌲 = GOOD SHORT HIKE ALSO AVAILABLE

NOTE: This guidebook is intended for use by competent hikers who accept the inherent and sometimes unpredictable hazards associated with the activity. Read the introduction and be sure of your ability to safely hike any of the trails listed <u>before</u> venturing out. **The user assumes all risks!**

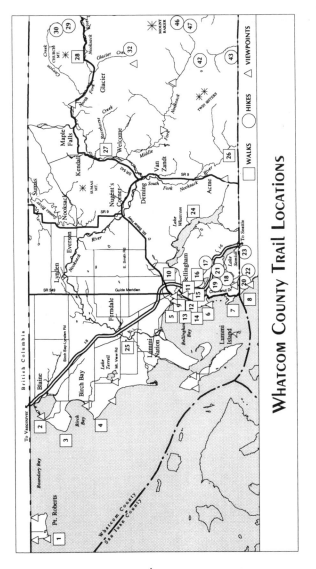

# WHATCOM COUNTY TRAIL LOCATIONS

□ WALKS  ○ HIKES  △ VIEWPOINTS

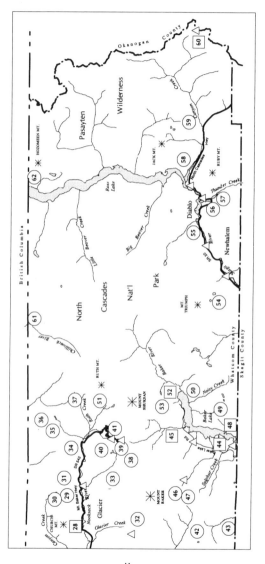

# Introduction

It is a delight to explore on foot the surprising diversity in nature found in Whatcom County, Washington. Numerous parks and hundreds of miles of trails provide access to storm-sculpted rocky shorelines, rain-shadow beaches, lowland fields and flowers, lakes, streams, verdant forests, waterfalls, and breathtaking alpine meadows, glaciers and towering peaks of the North Cascades, making this one of the most interesting regions in Northwest America in which to walk.

This guidebook offers a wide selection of trails, including easy walks and more strenuous hikes throughout the county. Many areas are accessible year round. An emphasis has been given to trails in the lowlands and the Mt. Baker area that aren't well described elsewhere, although much more is included. While many offer overnight possibilities, all are presented as day hikes. Listings of some of the more significant public parks, viewpoints and campgrounds around the county are also provided.

## About Whatcom County

On a line north to south, Whatcom County spans barely 25 miles, though its western coastline touches over 130 miles of saltwater. The land stretches 115 miles west to east from the Pt. Roberts peninsula to Harts Pass at the crest of the Cascades Range. Three fourths of the land area is rugged mountain wilderness, as rugged and remote as anywhere in the lower forty-eight states. Nearly all 140,000+ inhabitants live in the western "lowlands" within 15 miles of Georgia Strait (or "Northern Puget Sound" or "Salish Sea," as some people call these waters). The lowlands consist of 200,000 acres of glacial outwash called Whatcom Basin. A mile-thick sheet of ice more than once covered the region, finally receding northward just a few thousand years ago. Great meltwater streams, predecessors of the Fraser and Nooksack Rivers, dumped their sediments here to form this huge rolling delta.

In a short time, geologically speaking, the land was densely forested and later occupied (or reoccupied) by native American tribes, including the Lummi and Nooksack people. Only 140 years ago, white settlers arrived at Bellingham Bay to harvest old-growth timber and mine sizeable deposits of coal, at the same time forcing the natives to confine themselves to bits of land west, north and east of Bellingham. Despite the moist marine climate, remote locale and recurring economic ups and downs, these hardy American and European pioneers ("intruders" would be less polite) adapted well to the challenge. The Nooksack River was made navigable, forestry and agricultural communities rapidly emerged upstream, the wooded floodplains were converted to prime farmland, large fish canneries were built, and secondary industries sprung up to tie them all together. (Remarkable and detailed histories of the region are preserved on many dusty pages found on the shelves of most local libraries.)

Now, much of these tamed pastoral lowlands are devoted to agriculture, supporting one of the largest milk-producing counties in the nation. That which isn't farmed, or developed into cities, towns and rural homesteads is almost entirely forested or otherwise managed for timber production. Agriculture, fishing, oil refining, aluminum production, mall shopping, tourism, higher education (Western Washington University), and a somewhat frazzled wood products industry, are among the fatter jacks of the local economy. This economy is becoming more diversified as new people and

businesses immigrate to the area, attracted largely by the quality of life here. But that cherished *quality of life*—pastoral country-side, forested open space, quiet lakes, beaches, small town ambiance, clean water, unclogged streets and lonely trails—isn't what it used to be. Southern California-style growth and development (they said it couldn't happen here) is clogging the landscape north of Bellingham and elsewhere. Strangely enough, a few developers, land speculators, politicians, and leaders of the local property rights crusade have many rural folks up in arms—not about what poor planning can do to the rural lifestyle, but over the right to make Whatcom County a growth and development free-for-all. It's a confused time, to be sure.

South and east of Whatcom Basin, the lowlands rise several thousand feet into foothills: 300,000 acres of little mountains heavily forested with second and third generation timber. Sumas and Vedder Mountains lift the horizon to the northeast, while a unique series of foothills straddling the Whatcom/Skagit County line extends all the way from the jaggy peaks of the North Cascades to saltwater at Chuckanut Mountain—the only place in the Cascade Range where its foothills touch the marine shore. The South Fork Nooksack River and Lake Whatcom further shape the complexity of this geographic anomaly (for more information, write to the **North Cascades Corridor Project**, PO Box 4003, Bellingham, WA 98227). The Northwest coastal forest of the foothills and lowlands is dominated by douglas fir, western hemlock and western red cedar thriving in a lush bed of ferns, berries, vines and numerous forest wildflowers. Predominant hardwoods include red alder, birch, big leaf maple and cottonwood. Wildlife populations are diverse, ranging from delicate and elusive amphibians, small and medium furry mammals up to large black bears, elk, deer, cougar and mountain goats. Bird species residing in or passing through the county number in the hundreds.

A significant rural human population (not all of them whacky about property rights) inhabits the lower slopes of the foothills and adjacent valley bottoms. Some of the present small communities are the remnants of bustling mill towns and marketing centers of a colorful past. Much of the foothills, however, is owned in large blocks by the state and by private timber companies and is managed primarily for timber production. Hundreds of miles of trails and logging roads wind through this shadowy landscape offering potential access to hikers, hunters, off-road vehicles and, of course, chainsaws. In some areas, logging clearcuts, old and new, have had an obvious impact on views and the environment... the ugly price we pay for big houses, telephone poles and paper on which to print books. Nevertheless, great views, wildlife, lakes, waterfalls and other sights are hidden here. While large areas are generally accessible to the public and some outstanding portions of this great forest have been preserved as parks, many areas are not open to the public. (Don't trespass!)

Nestled among the hills are four major lakes, all with developed public park facilities: Lake Padden, Silver Lake (camping), Lake Samish, and the largest, Lake Whatcom (5,000 acres). The higher elevations are found on Lookout, Stewart, Blue and Sumas Mountains; all are under 3,500 feet above sea level. Just south of Bellingham is Chuckanut Mountain, composed of 60 million-year-old fossilized sandstone. This area contains a superb marine state park (Larrabee) with camping facilities and many popular hiking trails leading to quiet lakes, rocky shores and scenic viewpoints. The Nooksack River, with its three forks and extensive tributary system drains a respectable watershed encompassing most of the western half of Whatcom County, including the north and west flanks of Mt. Baker. A few streams flow north into Canada and the Fraser River.

Beyond the foothills lies the sprawling glacial-carved wilderness of the northern Cascade Range. These federally managed lands comprise about two-thirds of the county's 1.4 million acres. Well over a half million acres of magnificent wildlands are protected for future generations as National Park and National Wilderness Areas, including the spectacular alpine country surrounding the 10,778 foot Mt. Baker volcano. Ice-clad and steaming, this great landmark dominates the horizon as far away as Seattle and Victoria. Edmond Coleman first reached the summit of "Koma Kulshan" in August, 1868 and now more than a thousand ascents may occur during each summer season.

Other high peaks often exceed 8,000 feet, and are flanked by extensive glaciers, alpine meadows, lakes and virgin forests. Three large reservoirs, Ross, Diablo and Baker Lakes occupy roughly 20,000 acres in the Skagit and Baker River valleys. Another 200 lakes, most above 3,000 feet, can also be found in the North Cascades of Whatcom County. Skagit County to the south is a similar wonderland in many respects and like Snohomish, Chelan and Okanogan Counties, is unsurpassed in its wild mountain beauty and diverse landscape.

Unfortunately, all this beauty and diversity cannot easily protect itself from the uncertain whims of humanity. Society must act together to fend off potential abusers. To that end, one of the more interesting park and wilderness proposals to come along in awhile is the *Cascades International Park*. This citizen-driven effort is focused on an area that includes existing parks and preserves on both sides of the international boundary as well as some new protected areas that, together, can help ensure the long-term viability of the greater North Cascades ecosystem. (For more information on this worthy cause, write to the *Northwest Ecosystems Alliance, P. O. Box 2813, Bellingham, WA 98227.*)

## Climate & Season

Although prospectors and surveyors were blazing trails into the North Cascades a century ago, few roads pierce this stronghold of nature. Development has been limited by precipitous terrain–and a lot of precipitation (mostly snow). Except for a few low elevation trails along the Nooksack, Skagit and Baker rivers, most hiking areas are buried in deep snow six months out of the year. As much as 150 inches of water, including about twenty feet of snow, falls on Mt. Baker annually. This compares to 35-40 inches at Bellingham (mostly rain) and 60 or more inches in the foothills. To the east, from Ross Lake to the Cascade crest (the eastern county line), 50 to 75 inches fall, almost entirely in the form of snow. The extreme eastern portion of the county is drier, but virtually unknown among most of the population. It is a high and wide open mountain wilderness landscape, a big sky country flanked by forests of pine and fir. It is also four hours away by car from Bellingham (*see hike #58, Hart's Pass*).

The warm Pacific High usually dominates the summer weather over much of northwest Washington, while moist marine and dry arctic air masses compete to influence the weather during the rest of the year. The lowlands experience a mild (but moist) climate and remain reasonably accessible throughout the seasons. In the light breeze, springtime jaunts are ideal here while the Cascades are still snowed in. Hiking doesn't have to be limited to sunny days, as some might suppose. Beach walks are great any time, but beware of rising and falling tides, especially during stormy periods. The casual hiker, properly clothed and shod, will find a November sunset stroll along a windy shore can be just as enjoyable as

an April day hike up Chuckanut Mountain, or a cool October outing into the colorful Nooksack Cirque.

Nevertheless, in summer the flowering alpine meadows high in the North Cascades are especially inviting and difficult to surpass in their superb and inspiring beauty. July through September and sometimes June and October are the best months for good weather in the North Cascades. In heavy snow years, the higher trails may not even start to open up until July. Wildflowers and snowfields have all but disappeared by September, with fall colors peaking by early October.

Weather is often unpredictable, so good raingear is essential in the mountains. Many days of cold rain and/or gusty winds can be expected anywhere anytime with or without any warning. Thunder storms are not unusual, so avoid ridge tops, taller trees and open water if you think lightning may strike in the vicinity. Snow is possible any day of the year above 5,000 feet. HYPOTHERMIA, therefore, IS A MOST SERIOUS CONCERN, having claimed the lives of more than a few unprepared victims. In the lower elevations, if you're dressed for the weather, hiking season lasts all year.

## Wʜᴀᴛ Tᴏ Kɴᴏᴡ Bᴇғᴏʀᴇ Yᴏᴜ Gᴏ

Preparation

A rewarding trip is usually one with good prep: proper dress, adequate food and water, and a few other basic items in the rucksack. Unsolicited advise: tell someone where you're going and know your limits under the conditions around you. Sharpen your senses before and during your walk. Go at a comfortable pace and make it an enjoyable outing for yourself and your mates. Travel in a small group–three or four is ideal. Anticipate problems that might arise and prepare for them. Is the weather unstable? Will you return before dark? When does the tide come in? Will there be snow on the trail?

Many walks require little more preparation than what's needed to check the mail at the end of the drive. Some hikes require much more foresight, especially in remote destinations. Overnight trips are another matter altogether. This guide is not intended to prepare you for overnight backpacking trips, though many of the hikes listed offer great overnight possibilities. Consult the library, outdoor clubs (listed at the end of the book) and knowledgeable persons if you want to further your skills in wilderness camping and other backcountry adventures. Numerous books are available that provide specific information on clothing, equipment, navigation skills, camping, weather, ice axe use, hazards and other elements you may or may not be familiar with. Remember that trail conditions change due to any number of factors, so the trail descriptions in this book are not cast in concrete. Carry along a bucket of common sense.

## Some Rules

In the Cascades, check with the park or forest ranger for regulations, trail conditions and other details before arriving at the trailhead. On federal park and forest lands, a few rules need to be noted: keep the party size small, never more than twelve; practice "no trace" hiking and camping; don't trample or destroy vegetation by camping on it or short-cutting trails; pack out your garbage; control your pet (pets are not allowed within the National Park); and, avoid building fires outside of designated areas. Free backcountry permits are required in the National Park for overnight trips. Camp only in developed campsites and build fires only where specifically permitted, but carry a small backpack stove for cooking.

Some knowledge of first aid is highly recommended and essential when traveling in remote places. Beware of changing conditions and unseen hazards. Creek crossings can be dangerous during high runoff periods. Notice that streams often fall during the night and rise in the afternoon. In early season especially, avoid all steep open snow slopes, due to avalanche danger. If you're unsure, don't chance it. Stay on the trail and don't lose it.

*If you do get lost*, calling out, staying put, and marking your location so it's visible from the air may be your best options. Keep dry and exercise if needed to stay warm.

Sturdy, water-resistant lug-soled boots are recommended for mountain trails and on snow. Carry plenty of water. Stream or lake water must always be boiled or purified or you run an increasing risk of catching the giardia bug and other serious health maladies. On logging roads, watch out for large trucks hauling their heavy loads of timber off the mountain. Be cautious during hunting season (generally in the fall). Wear bright orange when large mammals are in season, or don't go.

Finally, exercise respect for other walkers, for wildlife and the environment. At home, take time on occasion to speak up for trails and wilderness. Before you and I arrived on the scene, others were doing that for us.

## Conditioning

The better shape you're in, the more enjoyable the hiking will be. And the best way to get in shape is to go for a hike! If you hike often, each trip better prepares you for the next, each becoming more and more effortless as you improve your conditioning. Most trips require only average physical condition. Maintain a comfortable pace. Check with your doctor if there's any doubt about your health or ability to make the trip. If you're not in the greatest shape, start with shorter walks and slowly work up to more strenuous hikes. Don't push yourself to the point that you are gasping for air or listening to your pulse pound in your head. This is supposed to fun. Take plenty of breaks, relax and enjoy the natural surroundings. Think, ponder, contemplate. Discover meaning in your hiking partner's life...

## Clothing & Equipment

For convenience, a suggested clothing and equipment list is included below. Volumes have been written on the selection and use of gear for a variety of hiking environments. Outdoor shops are excellent sources of information. Dressing comfortably means wearing loose-fitting layers that can be added or removed as necessary. Just being fashionable won't do. Feet need special attention. A boot that fits is mandatory. Thick socks over thin help absorb friction away from your skin. Under typical northwest skies, the best combination in the mountains often includes a fast-drying synthetic layer against the skin, a light wool shirt or sweater, wool or synthetic durable pants (avoid cotton), a heavy wool sweater or pile jacket, and a wind and water-resistant shell, top and bottom.

Wet clothes can result in a rapid and dangerous loss of body heat. Add layers, gloves, a hat and parka in colder weather. Nights in the mountains, even in summer, are usually cold. A wool hat that pulls down over the ears makes a great thermostat. Put it on before you start shivering and remove it before you sweat. Effective, fashionable sunglasses and sun cream (SPF 15 or better) are appropriate for bright days, cloudy days in the snow, and hot tub parties.

For short day trips, a hip or fanny pack may be useful to carry food and drink, a nature guide, camera, windbreaker, etc. A rucksack will be required for mountain trips. Some of the higher trails can still be snow-covered in summer and an ice axe and the ability to use it may be necessary for safety. Contact outdoor shops or clubs to learn proper ice axe technique. Any number of other items can be carried as well. In remote areas, care must be taken to avoid getting caught in darkness or bad weather without the essentials in your rucksack. Study the following list and notice what other experienced hikers carry with them.

*Short walks:*

Food, water, proper clothing, footwear, camera, binoculars, guidebook, sunglasses, sun cream.

*Short hikes:*

Same as above, and sturdy lug-soled boots, small pack, extra clothing (sweater, raingear), pocket knife, whistle, flashlight, batteries, first aid kit.

*Longer dayhikes:*

Same as above, and extra food and water, more clothes and raingear, map & compass (learn to use it), matches, fire-starter, foam pad, toilet paper, insect repellent, emergency shelter.

For those who may be "hiking" by wheelchair (let's hear it for accessible trails!), modify the list as needed.

## Backcountry Sanitation

Cleaning yourself or your food containers and cook pots should always occur well away from water sources. Use common sense if you need to make a nature call. Get well off the trail and a good distance—100 feet or more—from streams or water bodies. Dig a shallow hole into the humus soil layer then cover it up well. If it's safe (damp and raining), burn your toilet paper. Leaves or snow work well if you forget the TP. Whenever possible, take care of these little duties before you hit the trail.

## Private Property

Veteran hikers in the county may notice that several classic lowland trails are not included in the book. This is not because the author missed them, but rather they traverse private lands whose owners do not wish to advertise their use by the general public. Liability for injures, vandalism and fires are common concerns (owners often don't realize, however, that they are well protected from liability by state law). A few careless people appear to be responsible for most public access problems being experienced. Local residents, outdoor shops and park managers are possible sources to consult with in locating these secret places.

A lot of good hiking country is under private timber company ownership where access is sometimes a little easier. You can generally avoid trouble with these folks by obeying all signs, closed gates, fences, seasonal fire closures or other indications that your presence is not welcome. Obtain permission where necessary. Descriptions in this guide should not be construed as permission to violate private property rights. Always assume that camping and campfires are not permitted outside of designated sites.

As for your own private property–your personal valuables, that is–don't leave them in your car at trailheads. Way too many brainless thieves have a habit of showing up at the oddest hours to break a window and make off with your goods. Report thefts to the authorities.

Beach Access

It is often assumed that any old beach is open to the public. That is generally true in Oregon and Hawaii and other coastal states but not in Washington. Unfortunately, the State of Washington sold off its best tidelands to private interests over much of this century. Not only was it an absurd thing to do, it left us with major difficulties in finding good access to more than a tiny fraction of the county's spectacular shoreline. Fortunately, the practice was banned about twenty-five years ago, but the damage was done. There is still a legal argument, and the author agrees, that the public never gave up its right to use tidelands to access public waters, whether for commerce or recreation or whatever, even though the mud and the crud may belong to an adjacent landowner. All that said, private property still deserves some respect.

Private or otherwise, the vast majority of tideland owners are not snobs and couldn't care less whether you and I go for a harmless stroll along a remote beach. However, they are not inclined to advertise these places to the general public due, in part, to the problems caused by a few individuals who abuse the privilege. Obnoxious behavior, litter and vandalism are primary concerns, especially where waterfront homes are located close to the shore. Fortunately, remote areas are more interesting to visit and responsible hikers will encounter few problems with anxious landowners. On all beaches (public and private), use common sense: don't take or leave anything, don't start fires, be quiet, avoid large groups, respect wildlife and the marine environment, be courteous to residents and stay off the stairs and pathways leading up to their yards.

Beach walks may be good year-round, except during stormy periods. The suggested walks and hikes in coastal areas (#1 through #8) include those with public access, although both public and private tideland ownership may occur. Nevertheless, these areas have been used regularly by the public in the past. While it would take a title company and a survey crew to know for sure which areas are private, there are substantial public tidelands present. *It is the user's responsibility to obtain prior authorization if necessary.* Plan your visit during lower tide levels (check the tide tables) and be aware of rising tides which can surprise, strand and/or drown you if you're not careful. **Walk these and all other areas at your own risk!**

# How To Use This Book

To make best use of this guidebook, first read the introductory material, then decide on a walk or a hike. Check the key map for possibilities, read the trail descriptions, then check the map again for possible side trips in the vicinity.

On the key map (*p. xi-xii*) trails have been divided up (somewhat arbitrarily) into "walks" and "hikes" to reflect the level of difficulty one might expect to find. Walks are generally less than an hour or two round trip and are not especially steep or difficult. Hikes are more strenuous but vary greatly in length, steepness and overall difficulty. Of course, what may seem to one person to be an easy stroll may be a real workout for the next. Refer to the symbols on the key map. Round-trip (RT) distance (with options), approximate time, elevation gain, best months to visit (varies year to year), and directions from Bellingham or I-5, including mile-post (MP) notations, are provided for each listing. The estimated times are given for walking speeds of one to two miles per hour. Three miles per hour is brisk and four is almost a trot and difficult to maintain over much distance. Additional time is added where elevation gain is significant.

Trips are divided loosely into four geographical areas: Coastal Areas, the Lowlands, the area around Mt. Baker, and the North Cascades beyond Mt. Baker. A special emphasis has been given to walks and hikes which are not adequately described in other guidebooks. A number of other potential trips are mentioned at the end of the trail section, which are not described for a variety of reasons: limited space, lack of information, well covered by other guides, etc. A determined adventurer will soon cultivate the detective skills needed to locate these and other semi-secret trails.

Listings of public parks briefly describe the facilities available and may include short walks not listed elsewhere in the guide. Viewpoints are accessible by car, bike or a short walk and are self-explanatory. A list of public campgrounds is provided for those who might want to combine one or more day hikes with a comfortable evening in the woods. Maps are intended for general reference only. Far better full-sized topographical maps to all areas are available at many outdoor shops.

For More Information

Several guidebooks are presently available which provide comprehensive coverage of trails in the Cascades, most notably *100 Hikes in the North Cascades* (Spring, Manning/The Mountaineers, 1988/92), and *Hiking the North Cascades* (Darvill/Sierra Club, 1982). Both are available at most book stores and hiking shops in the region. Several local outdoor clubs sponsor guided hikes throughout the year, free of charge. These are listed at the end of the book along with emergency contacts and various land management agencies. Libraries are another excellent source of how-to and where-to hiking information.

# Coastal Areas

*(See note on beach walks, page 16.)*

# 1.    Lighthouse Point

*Walking distance: 0.5 - 1 mile RT*
*Time: Allow 1 hour*                    *Season: Year-round*

This short beach walk and visit to Lighthouse Marine Park are worth the trip to Point Roberts.  Amazingly, few mainland Whatcom Countians have ever been there.  Access is by way of Canada (*see Lighthouse Marine Park for directions*).  Once at the park, climb the view tower to see the Gulf and San Juan Islands, Vancouver Island, BC Ferries on Georgia Strait, and maybe gray or orca whales, both of whom are known to approach close to the beach.  The stroll along the beach needs no description.  Campsites are available (*info: 945-4911*).

Drive or bike around the Point to visit two border beaches: Boundary Bay to the east and Monument Park on the west (an undeveloped county park with a rough steep trail to the beach).  Both offer short walks: public tidelands are limited. The premier marine bluff in the county, Lily Point (southeast corner of the Point), is difficult to access.  Eroding bluffs 200 feet high feed the natural littoral drift process that builds beaches down-drift of the bluffs.  A rare grove of old-growth big-leaf maple lies nearby; archaeological and wildlife resources also exist. A major residential project is planned here, so future access is uncertain.

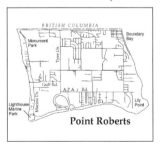

Point Roberts

*Old hull at Semiahmoo Spit.*

## 2.    Semiahmoo Spit

*Walking distance:  1 - 3 miles RT*
*Time:  Allow 1 - 2 hours*          *Season:  Year-round*

With so much of the marine tidelands under private ownership, it's hard to find a good public beach of any length to walk in Whatcom County.  The unique spit at Semiahmoo Park is therefore a real treasure, still somewhat undiscovered. A resort development at the north end of this 1.3 mile long back-to-back beach system (an "accretion shoreform"), attracts throngs of visitors in summer.  Visit the park in the off-season and you might have most of the spit to yourself. Breezy days in spring or fall and cool clear winter mornings are nicest.  This is also when many species of birds and other wildlife are more likely to be seen.

To reach the spit, take I-5 exit #274 to Portal Way, then immediately turn left on Blaine Rd. (*map, p. 24*).  In .7 mile go right on Drayton Harbor Rd., and follow signs to Semiahmoo, 4.5 miles from I-5.  From the park, walk either beach or a gravel path along the spit to the resort.   Cross the road and head back to the start.  The west beach can be followed to a point south of the boat launch where fallen trees and drift logs make the going tougher.  The views are great across Drayton Harbor toward Mt. Baker, and across Semiahmoo Bay to the city of Whiterock, B.C.  Some of the old buildings left over from the days of the historic Alaska Packers Association have been converted to interpretive facilities, a library and gift shop.  (*See the listing under Semiahmoo Park #3.*)

# 3.  Blaine Area

*Distance: 1 - 4 miles*
*Time: Allow 1 - 2 hours*          *Season: Year-round*

Two easy urban walks at Blaine include a scenic loop trail (about
a mile long) that parallels Semiahmoo Bay and Marine Dr., with
views, picnic sites, an amphitheater, an intriguing orca sculpture,
and at the west end of the harbor area, a nicely improved public
fishing dock. The historic footferry, MV Plover, makes frequent
summer runs to Semiahmoo Spit (free, but donations appreci-
ated). From the last I-5 exit before entering Canada, head west
then immediately go right on Marine Dr. to find the trail. Watch
for bay ducks and shorebirds. East of I-5 on the north side of H St.,
another short walk (0.5 mile) leads through a lovely conifer forest
at an oasis of nature called Lincoln Park. Trails are easy to follow.

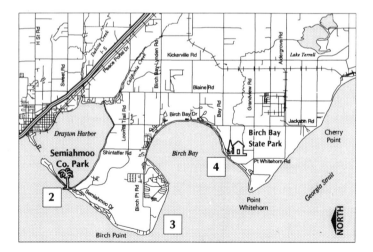

# 4.    Birch Bay To Cherry Point

*Hiking distance:  2 - 5 miles RT*
*Time:  Allow 1.5 - 4 hours*          *Season:  Year-round*

One of the best beach walks in the county, this trip is especially good for bird life–over 300 species have been counted at Birch Bay State Park.  Early in the year, take your bird book and binoculars and watch for bay and shore birds, including brant geese, american widgeons, scoters, harlequins, oldsquaws, loons, dunlin and others.  Huge flocks hang around in spring when the herring are spawning off shore.  Harbor seals may be found basking close to shore.  The San Juan Islands, Gulf Islands, and Vancouver Island dominate the west horizon. Some of the tidelands just south of the park are private; keep off the occasional paths and stairways and stay friendly.

From I-5 Exit #270, Birch Bay-Lynden Rd., head west four miles, turning left at the waterslides, then left again onto Birch Bay Dr. (*map, p. 24*). Reach the State Park in two miles (*camping available—see Birch Bay State Park #4*). Begin anywhere along the beach and wander southward toward Point Whitehorn in the distance. The beach graduates from sand and fine gravel to pebbles and cobbles farther south. Large boulders released from the high eroding bluffs are relics of the ice age that probably brought the material down from British Columbia as recently as 15,000 years ago. Northwest Coast Salish Indians occupied this area for many generations as evidenced by a shell midden. As the beach gradually bends 90 degrees to the left, Lummi Island becomes visible to the south-southeast. This is Point Whitehorn. You may want to consider turning back here (it's about a 35-45 minute walk from the south end of the park to this point).

For the longer beach hike, continue southeast at low tide another four miles to Cherry Point (arrange to leave a car or bike at the end of Gulf Rd. for the return trip). This section is mostly cobble beach and passes under the ARCO pier 1.2 mile before Gulf Rd. A small creek can be crossed on logs (or by wading) and a unique berm and backwater marsh appear in the last 1/4 mile. This southern segment has been and will continue to be a focus of controversy as developers and politicians press for more heavy industrial development in the vicinity. Hopefully, new industry will be sensitive to the environment and to the valuable wildlife and recreational resources that exist here.

*Little Squalicum Beach*

## 5. Little Squalicum Beach

*Walking distance:*        *1 - 4 miles RT*
*Time: Allow 1 - 3 hours*    *Season: Year-round*

This attractive gravely beach just north of Bellingham is littered with small relics from historic industry on Bellingham Bay. Old bricks and odd rusty contrivances add interest to a surprisingly scenic saunter. The beach is adjacent to the Little Squalicum ravine which could become one of the city's next parks. There are now three easy ways to reach the beach. Follow West Holly St. and Eldridge Ave. out of downtown Bellingham to Nequalicum St., immediately past the first bridge. Turn right then left on Nome. Either go left on W.

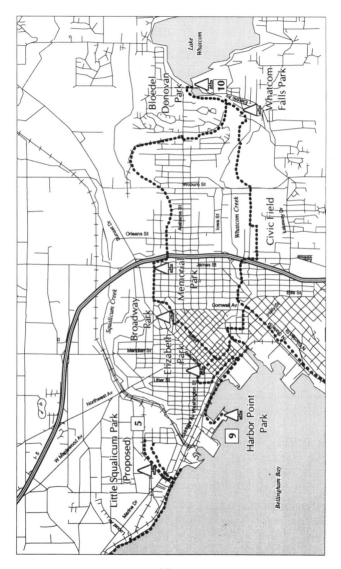

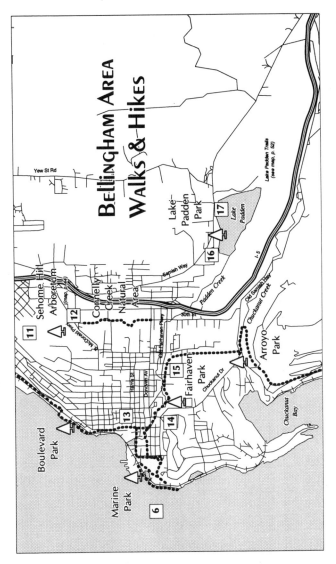

# Bellingham Area Walks & Hikes

Yew St Rd

Sehome Hill
Arboretum

(map, p. 44)

11

12 Connelly
Creek
Natural
Area

Lake
Padden
Park

17 Lake
Padden

Lake Padden Trails
(see map, p. 52)

Samish Way

16

I-5

Padden Creek

30th St

Old Samish Way

15

13

14 Fairhaven
Park

Chuckanut Creek

Arroyo
Park

Chuckanut Dr

Boulevard
Park

Marine
Park

6

Chuckanut
Bay

S. McConnell Pkwy

Old Fairhaven Pkwy

14th St

Knox Av

Maryland to the lower parking lot of the Bellingham Technical College (may be restricted), or go a block farther and left on Illinois (*map, page 28*). A boulder marks the trail at the end of the street. It's a 0.3 mile walk to the beach.

Or, from a low point of the BTC parking lot, walk through a gate and follow an unmarked trail through trees and meadow. Head for the overpass (Eldridge Ave.) and a gravel road that leads to a large railroad trestle at the water's edge. From either approach pass under the trestle to what was once one of Bellingham's best swimming beaches. Pollution from industry and residential septic systems put an end to that, although improved enforcement of regulations could lead to a reopening of Whatcom County's own Waikiki. For now head right under a pier (someday, this could become the west terminus of the Bay-To-Baker Trail). Follow the beach to a pipeline where the walk ends if the tide's up. The next section passes below the old Columbia Cement plant. Beyond, the hike becomes much more interesting. Watch for eagles in perch trees above the shore. About a half-mile from the pier, just before a cluster of old pilings, a short new trail leads up a draw to Locust Ave. west of Marine Dr., the third access to the beach (a lack of parking makes this trailhead less appealing). Depending on conditions, one may be able to continue north to the old Fort Bellingham site near the mouth of the Nooksack River four miles away. Exits to Marine Dr. are scarce and difficult. If there's enough support, the County might be willing to develop a small viewpoint and nature trail at the north end of the beach adjacent to the Nooksack estuary.

# 6. Post Point

*Walking distance:*      *I mile RT*
*Time: Allow I hour*      *Season: Year-round*

From Marine Park at the west end of Harris Ave. in Fairhaven, this short popular walk follows the beach and railroad tracks (use caution) south to Post Point (*map, page 29*). At lower tides, it's a pleasant half-mile stroll one way to the low-lying rocky point in the distance. Continuing farther is not recommended since it could be difficult to get out of the way of a passing train. In winter, hundreds, maybe thousands of ducks, scoters, and grebes, mergansers, and a few loons, eagles and kingfishers can be seen. Even a grey whale, though rarely seen in Bellingham Bay, is not unheard of. This walk can be combined with the Padden Creek Trail (*see walk #14*).

*Rocky shore at Larrabee State Park.*

# 7.  Larrabee State Park

*Walking distance:*          *0.5 - 1 mile RT*
*Time:  Allow 1 hour*       *Season:  Year-round*

The stormswept rocky shore at Larrabee State Park is one of the more wild and scenic places in western Whatcom County. Eroded 60 million year-old sandstone lines the water's edge, capped by evergreen forests of douglas fir and madrone.  The beaches and tide pools below invite curious kids and adults to experience marine ecology close-up among communities of starfish, mussels, barnacles, crabs and anemones.  The park is the state's oldest and offers exceptional opportunities for hiking, camping (including walk-in sites), kayaking, wildlife viewing, picnicking and photography.

To sample this intriguing landscape, drive 5 miles south of Fairhaven or bike the Interurban Trail (*hike #15*) to the park's main parking lot south of the campground. Walk down a path left of the bandstand and through a short tunnel beneath the railroad tracks. Stairs lead down to an easy trail that follows the shore a short distance north and south. Go left 150 yards to a rocky point and one of the loveliest waterfront views in the region, marred only by the misplaced construction of a house at Whiskey Rock. At the junction below the tunnel, go right 100 yards to a fine beach, popular in summer. If the tide is way out, you can wander the beach and sandstone outcrops a bit more to the giant rock wall and boat launch on Wildcat Cove. This is a popular launch for kayaks, while the rock wall attracts roped climbers.

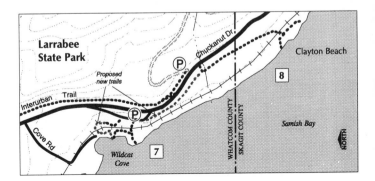

33

*Samish Bay pocket beach.*

# 8. Clayton Beach

*Hiking distance:*        1.5 - 2 miles RT
*Time: Allow 1 - 2 hours*    *Season: Year-round*

Clayton Beach is an outstanding addition to Larrabee State Park that came about in the late 1980s as a direct result of grass roots citizen action to save the area from development. Much of the credit goes to Puget Sounders, a regional environmental education group based in Bellingham. The area has been used by the public for many years, but is expected to draw much larger numbers in the future. Development plans by state park officials have been controversial: a new service road, pedestrian bridge over the tracks, restrooms and other facilities are planned. Care must be taken to ensure that the tranquillity and wilderness character of the beach–the same qualities that fueled the citizen effort to save the area–are not compromised.

To access the beach, park at a new parking area just south of the south entrance to Larrabee Park (*map, page 33*). Cross the highway (caution here), descend stairs and head left on the old Interurban grade through forest and possible mud to a short, steep rock slab. Scramble down (slippery) and cross the railroad tracks when safe (a new trail and pedestrian overpass may exist by the time you read this). Follow the path to the water's edge where unique sandstone formations mark the north end of a broad sandy beach. Low tides allow much exploring north and south. Adventurous hikers may be able to scramble northward along the shore the long way back to the main park area (*see walk #7*).

# Lowland Trails

*Lady ferns.*

# 9.  Squalicum Harbor/Historic B'ham

*Walking distance:  3.5 miles*      *Time: Allow  2 - 4 hours*
*Elevation gain:  200 feet*      *Season:  Year-round*

One of two walking tours of Bellingham, the emphasis here is on historic buildings in the downtown area and in the Columbia neighborhood.    Squalicum Harbor, lower Whatcom Falls, a fish hatchery, a museum, two parks and a lot of beautiful century-old Victorian homes exist along the route.  In the residential areas, keep an eye on all the chimneys: no two look quite the same.

Beginning at Harbor Point Park (*see park #9*) or at the parking lot immediately north of the Harbor Center, walk along the inner harbor then cut left to Roeder Avenue and head downtown (*map, page 28*).  Pass the collapsing grass-covered Citizens Dock (built in 1913 as a passenger and freight terminal), then turn left on Central Ave.  Cross W. Holly, enter Maritime Heritage Park and follow the paved path along Whatcom Creek.  For a side trip, take the path and stairs up the hill to visit the 1892 French Victorian Whatcom Museum of History and Art.  This landmark building was once City Hall for the town of New Whatcom and later Bellingham. Continuing along the creek, follow the path past viewpoints and benches to a foot bridge below the falls. (To reach the civic center and library, continue under the Prospect St. bridge along the creek to Grand Ave.  Eventually, the city plans to extend a trail system up the creek all the way to Whatcom Falls Park and Lake Whatcom (*see hike #10.*)

*Harbor Point Park & Squalicum Harbor*

Cross the footbridge to the hatchery and interpretive center then head uphill on a diagonal walkway to the west. This is the Old Village Trail. Pass the ancient Pickett house (1856) on the way to H. St. Jog to the right, then left at the striking Theater Guild building to reach Broadway and Elizabeth Park. Walk through the park (donated by the famous settler, Captain Henry Roeder in 1883) to the corner of Walnut and Washington, heading west on the latter. In the Columbia Neighborhood, many historic homes have been beautifully renovated. Watch for identifying plaques, but respect the residents' privacy. Turn left on Utter St. to see the attractive Shields House (1895) and the Loggie House (1893), whose early owner operated the largest cedar mill in the world in the

1920's. His daughter, Helen was a well known Pacific Northwest artist. Continue on Utter past the Countryman houses (1897, 1901), turning left at Eldridge Ave. (or keep exploring the neighborhood).

The Jenkins House at 1807 Eldridge was owned by the postmaster and father of a mayor of New Whatcom. Pass St. Paul's Episcopal Church at 2116 Walnut Street (built in 1884 for $1,300). There is a good view of Squalicum Harbor off the end of Broadway at West Holly St. (a view tower and sky bridge over the railroad tracks could happen here some day). Continue down Holly past the Aftermath Club (1905), a meeting place for women active in social and intellectual pursuits. Pass the First Baptist Church building (1311 I St.), the oldest church in Bellingham, and the Lottie Roth Block, a great example of Chuckanut sandstone construction.

Turn left on E St. to see the oldest brick building north of San Francisco. Built in 1858, the Richards Building (1308 E. St.) has been a general store, bank, warehouse, courthouse, jail, post office, taxidermy, newspaper company, outdoor equipment store, wood shop and who knows what else over its long life. Go back across West Holly to the old Great Northern Freight Depot, a long white building at E St. and Roeder Ave. Walk south and notice the attractive brick depot nearby. Walk to C St., turn right and right again on Roeder to return to Squalicum Harbor and complete the loop.

*Stone bridge at Whatcom Falls Park.*

# 10. Whatcom Creek

*Distance: 2 or 9 mile loop*  *Time: Allow 1 - 5 hours*
*Elevation gain: 100 - 400 feet*  *Season: Year-round*

Trails along Whatcom Creek—perhaps Bellingham's best-loved natural gem—offers several easy to moderate walks of a few miles or less, to a nine-mile loop from Lake Whatcom to Bellingham Bay and back. The longer loop combines trails and street sections, passes through seven parks, and touches the estuary at Bellingham Bay before returning via the Railroad Trail up Alabama Hill (or hop on a bus). An extensive trail system between Bloedel Donovan Park and Whatcom Falls Park offers a variety of loops past wetlands, wildlife ponds, waterfalls, time-sculpted sandstone, tall trees, a fish hatchery, and picnic areas. "Whatcom," a native term suggesting "noisy waters," is a perfect moniker for this wild urban creek as it descends more than 300 feet in four miles, right through the heart of Bellingham.

Regrettably, tragedy struck the Whatcom Creek corridor June 10, 1999 when Olympic Pipeline Company's underground fuel pipeline ruptured at Whatcom Falls Park, resulting in a catastrophic explosion that took the lives of three young people and destroyed a mile and a half of riparian and aquatic habitat, hundreds of trees, and tens of thousands of fish, birds, mammals, amphibians and other wildlife. The grief will be with us for a very long time, yet a major restoration effort is underway to assist in the recovery of the Whatcom Creek ecosystem. It is, therefore, especially important that trail users stay on the trail and avoid all closed areas.

Despite the damage, much remains that is well worth exploring. For either loop begin at Bloedel-Donovan Park at the north end of

Lake Whatcom (*map, p. 28*). Walk a few yards north on Electric Ave. to find the trailhead across the street. Formerly a railroad grade serving coal mines and sawmills on Lake Whatcom, the trail passes bird-rich Scudder Pond (thanks to the Audubon Society and Mrs. Armitage). Walk 0.2 mile past the pond to a wide trail merging from the left. Take it, then angle down and right on a narrower trail that quickly leads to another old railroad grade (a dilapidated trestle hovers like an old dream 30 yards to the left). Turn right on this grade, walk until a noisy waterfall comes into view, then go left down a path with steps. Continue downstream past a smaller waterfall, then the real Whatcom Falls above an exquisite stone bridge. For a short two-mile loop, cross the bridge and go left on a paved road past the fish hatchery to a path along the right side of a kids' fishing pond; take this to Electric Ave., cross and walk the last bit of trail to the starting point.

For the longer 4.5-mile hike to the bay, don't cross the stone bridge. Keep walking downstream to a wooden footbridge leading to an unpaved road (before crossing, walk a few yards more for a good view of the "whirlpool;" to see the area burned in the 1999 explosion, continue on this path, climb a flight of steps, turn left and left again on a new 0.5 mile path to the overlook). A new trail system is planned along Whatcom Creek from here all the way to the bay, but in the meantime an alternative is to cross the wooden bridge, turn right and continue straight ahead on road and trail for several hundred yards to Bayview Cemetery and a good view of the city. This path ends at the intersection of Woburn and Fraser Streets. Head left (uphill) on Woburn 0.3 mile, then go right on Wildflower Way. Walk down a block to another path; follow this and stay right to reach a bridge over a small creek. Cross to another quiet street, Toledo Ct., and follow it one block to more trail on the right. Walk this, then stay left to cross another bridge; go right at the next junction, and cross the street at the Frank Geri ballfields. Walk the obvious paved path west to Moore St. Another jog left and jog right brings you to Lincoln St. Turn right on Lincoln (becomes Meador) and follow this to State St. Cross to Kansas and in two blocks go right on Ellis. Walk a few yards and look to your left for a wide trail marked by two boulders and two fences. Follow this across Whatcom Creek to York St. Go right four blocks (becomes Flora) then right on Grand Ave. to City Hall and the Library grounds. Just north of Lottie St. take the stairs and path left off Grand. A paved path along lower Whatcom Creek passes Lower Whatcom Falls and ends at Maritime Heritage Park at the mouth of Whatcom Creek. There are many variations to try all along the route. (*See walks #9 and #13 for other options.*)

For the return loop to Bloedel Donovan Park from Maritime Heritage Park, take the Old Village Trail (the inclined sidewalk near the fish rearing ponds) north to H St. Turn right, pass the Theater Guild and stay on H St. past Fouts Park all the way to Logan St. Go left, then right on Broadway and right on S. Park Dr. Follow Broadway Park for several blocks then go left on Lyle St. and right on E. Illinois. Walk seven blocks to King St. and the north end of Memorial Park. Head rightward through lawn and trees toward the far southeast corner of the park and a short path leading to a footbridge across the freeway. From here the Railroad Trail is followed all the way up Alabama Hill. Cross Alabama St. to find the trail slightly downhill. This trail comes out parallel to Vining St., crosses Rhododendron and reenters Whatcom Falls Park. Either follow this to Electric Ave. where you began the hike, or take the return route for the shorter loop described above. Then go have an ice cream.

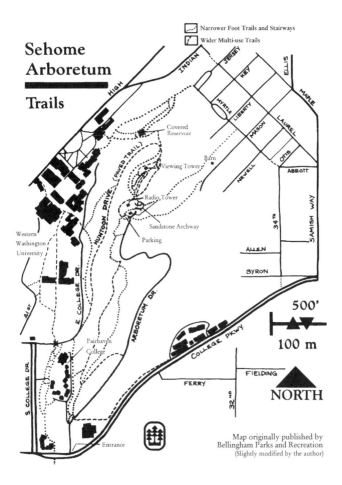

**Sehome Arboretum Trails**

⋯⋯ Narrower Foot Trails and Stairways

▱ Wider Multi-use Trails

HIGH

INDIAN

JERSEY

KEY

ELLIS

MAPLE

MYRTLE

LIBERTY

MIXON

LAUREL

NEWELL

OTIS

ABBOTT

SAMISH WAY

34TH

Covered Reservoir

Barn

Viewing Tower

Radio Tower

Sandstone Archway

Parking

HUNTOON DRIVE (PAVED TRAIL)

Western Washington University

ARBORETUM DR.

ALLEN

BYRON

21ST

E. COLLEGE DR.

Fairhaven College

COLLEGE PKWY.

500'

⊢■▲▼⊣

100 m

S. COLLEGE DR.

FERRY

32ND

FIELDING

▲ **NORTH**

Entrance

Map originally published by
Bellingham Parks and Recreation
(Slightly modified by the author)

# 11. Sehome Hill Arboretum

*Hiking distance:* 2 mile loop     *Time:* Allow 1 - 2 hours
*Elevation gain:* 250 feet     *Season:* Year-round

This hike near Western Washington University features a 165 acre natural arboretum, sandstone outcrops, a tunnel, and a view tower overlooking the city (*see viewpoint #10*). Sehome Hill was logged off at the turn of the century, becoming a city park and nature preserve some years later. Douglas fir seems to be overpowering the opportunistic hardwoods, stealing their sunlight, and promising ongoing ecological change in the forest community. There are several means of access and a number of side trails and short loops that can be explored. One can also combine the walk with a tour of the outdoor museum (sculptures) at the university (call ahead for information or explore on your own). To avoid throngs of students, try weekends or late afternoons.

From Samish Way, take Bill McDonald Pkwy to the first right after the high school. Follow this road 3/4 mile to the parking lot. Save the view for later. Instead, look for a sign pointing to "WWU" and follow the gravel path left along the west side of the parking lot (opposite the radio tower). The path (Douglas Fir Lane) winds gently down through an interesting mix of douglas fir, big leaf maple, sword ferns, red elderberry, snowberry and salal. Stay on the main trail, bypassing several forks that branch to the left. A four-way intersection appears about 10-15 minutes from the start; go straight. (The path to the right offers a shortcut to the return trail.) The main path curves sharply to the left, passing low sandstone cliffs popular

45

with rock climbers, before reaching the road 0.7 mile from the start. (By 1997, a new trail at this location may link Sehome Hill to the Connelly Creek Nature Area.)

At the road, turn right and then right again in 200 yards, just outside the gate, and follow the path up a couple of steps and left on the better trail. Soon, pass the shortcut route coming down from the right and continue to an intersection with a campus road; take the path on the right. Beyond, several spur trails access the university and its historic buildings, sculptures and landscape. The mostly paved trail (Sword Fern Lane) gradually rises through mixed forest and understory including red alder, big leaf maple, oregon grape, salal, oceanspray and a variety of ferns and wildflowers (in spring and early summer). Try to distinguish as many different plants as you can. If you don't know their names, make some up then look them up later. Just past a wide flat

of pavement, take the second right, a paved fork rising the last 180 yards to the view tower. The view of the city, bay and harbor is impressive: Vancouver Island, the Gulf Islands, Canadian peaks, Mt. Baker and part of the North Cascades are all visible on a good day. From the tower head right on a paved path leading back through a tunnel to the parking lot.

# 12. Connelly Creek Trail

*Walking distance: 1 - 6 miles RT*    *Time: Allow 1 - 4 hours*
*Elevation gain: Minimal*    *Season: Year-round*

This trail system through Bellingham's Happy Valley is gradually being expanded and improved. New trails will link the Connelly Creek Nature Area with Sehome Hill to the north and the Interurban Trail to the south (*map, p. 29*). From the new trailhead on Ferry Ave. near Sehome High School, walk south through forest and Joe's Garden, crossing 30th St. at Douglas Ave. Continue south to a small flood control dam then meander through woods, crossing Connelly Creek on bridges at several points. At a junction, go left then right to reach Donovan Ave. When built, the link to Interurban Trail

will go right along Donovan then left on the 28th St. right-of-way to Old Fairhaven Pkwy. The northern link to Sehome Hill will pass by Sehome High School and meander west to Bill McDonald Pkwy. and the arboretum. An unusual grove of Sitka spruce, extensive wetlands, and diverse wildlife habitat within the Nature Area make Connelly one of the City's more valuable greenway corridors.

# 13. South Bay Trail

*Walking distance: 1 - 6 miles RT*  *Time: Allow 1 - 4 hours*
*Elevation gain: None*  *Season: Year-round*

Bellingham's longest waterfront trail and greenway system, the South Bay Trail is still being developed. The corridor is a recreational and nonmotorized travel link between Fairhaven and the Interurban Trail to the south, and downtown and the Whatcom Creek Trail to the north (*map, p. 28*).

Beginning at 10th St. and Harris Ave. in Fairhaven, walk north to the obvious trail which leads to another short section of 10th St. and, in two blocks, the south entrance to Boulevard Park. Take the main trail through the park and down to a new crossing of the railroad tracks (use caution). Climb stairs over a steep rocky point above the tiny beach at "Easton Cove" to a wide trail following an old railroad grade through Boulevard Park. (Or, walk the new pier– if it's been built–it was still in the planning stages in 1996.) Continue north on a trestle and paved trail along the water's edge to a view tower and bridge over the tracks. Climb the tower for a good look yonder and cross the bridge to a sharp left on another paved path. Continue straight ahead, then go left at a fork and down to the lower unpaved trail. Follow this about a mile to the impressive Wharf St. trestle, passing several stairways allowing access to the Boulevard, South Hill and the university area (at Pine street). Take the new bicycle/ pedestrian trestle to Laurel St. and jog left to a new path to Railroad Ave. Follow the latter to York St. and the new bridge over Whatcom Creek at the trail's end.

# 14. Padden Creek & Bellingham Bay

*Walking distance: 1 - 5 miles RT*     *Time: Allow 1 - 4 hours*
*Elevation gain: 200 feet*     *Season: Year-round*

The hike along the lower reach of Padden Creek on Bellingham's southside is one of the nicer gems in the city trail system. Kudos to those who made it happen. The route offers several destinations and connects with other urban routes described in the book (*map, p. 28*).

From the tennis courts at Fairhaven Park, walk down the steps and go left along Padden Creek, crossing it three times on foot bridges (before the third, a path on the left leads up to the rose garden). At a four-way junction go left (straight ahead leads to 14th St. and right leads to the Interurban Trail). Continue, walking under the bridge you probably drove across, then pass a fish ladder at the outlet of a couple of unfriendly (to fish) culverts. Round the old 10th and Donovan intersection and take the trail back down into the canyon. The next section contours along the creek through a multi-layered canopy of trees and shrubs, passing a historic marker on the way. Diverse habitat opportunities exist for a variety of birds, amphibians and small mammals. Cross the creek and stay left (right goes to Padden Lagoon). Pass a marsh, continue across 6th and 4th Streets and head left at the sewer plant (right goes to the Alaska Ferry terminal). Take either fork ahead to explore the new loop trail then head north to Harris Avenue. Turn left to reach Marine Park, or right to Old Fairhaven. At 10th and Harris, walk south on 10th to find a short path leading back to Padden Creek Trail and Fairhaven Park.

# 15. Interurban Trail

*Walking distance: 3-6 miles (1-way)   Time: Allow 2 - 6 hours*
*Elevation gain: 200 feet                    Season: Year-round*

The Interurban trolley was the first mass transit system between Bellingham, Mt. Vernon and points south. Now, the route is used by hikers and bicyclists coming and going between Fairhaven, Arroyo Park, Larrabee State Park, and other areas in the Chuckanuts. Begin near the tennis courts at Fairhaven Park (or any of a number of other access points; *map, p. 29*). The path is generally wide and well maintained.

From the tennis courts take a wide gravel path through lawn which curves to the north then turn right on another wide path. Continue east on trails and a short section of sidewalk to 22nd St. Follow a new trail to the original trailhead off Old Fairhaven Pkwy. Turn to the south through forest and wetlands, crossing Old Samish Hwy (switchbacks) to Arroyo Park in about 1.5 mile. The trail drops down to a bridge over Chuckanut Creek and a good turn-around point for the shorter walk. Cross the bridge and climb to the old original grade where a large trestle once spanned the valley. Continue across California Street, pass a junction leading down to Teddy Bear Cove, then hike a long stretch to where the trail turns west, dips, and crosses the creek draining Fragrance Lake. Keep walking to intersect the Fragrance Lake Trail at Larrabee State Park (about 5 miles to here). Walk down to the right to reach Larrabee State Park or go straight ahead to find the Clayton Beach Trail (*see hike #8*).

# 16. Lake Padden I

*Walking distance:*       *2.6 mile loop*
*Time: Allow 1 - 2 hours*    *Season: Year-round*

The 2.6 mile trail around Lake Padden is popular year-round
with walkers and joggers (*see hike #17 for a 6-mile loop*). From
Bellingham, drive or peddle south on Samish Way about two
miles from I-5. Take either of two entrances into the park and
find the path near the lake (*see also Lake Padden Park*). Hike
either direction and generally follow the main trail closest to
the lake. The trail is in good condition and needs little
description. The north shore is low-lying and level. The south
shore involves a few easy hills and is heavily wooded. For
information on other trails in the area, look for a large trail
map near the mouth of Ruby Creek by the ballfields.

# 17.  Lake Padden II

*Hiking distance:*         *6 mile loop*
*Time:  Allow 3 - 4 hours*   *Season:  Year-round*

In addition to the popular loop trail around Lake Padden, a number of other trails exist along the ridge between the lake and I-5.  To get acquainted with some of these higher trails consider the following loop.  The trails are popular with mountain bikers and equestrians, both of whom have contributed to trail damage in the area in recent years.  Nevertheless, serious efforts are underway to rebuild the trail system which should make it much more suitable for all users. A number of spur trails can be explored along the way.  (*See walk #16 for directions to the park.*)  The city eventually plans to link the Lake Padden area with Connelly Creek and the Interurban Trail.

From the tennis courts, head right along the lakeshore, cross Padden Creek and walk uphill to a junction of two wide paths; stay right.  At a four-way junction at the ridge crest turn left (the other options are of more interest to people on horseback). Ups and downs lead 1/4 mile to another junction with a wide path; turn right (left returns to the lower lake loop).  The next section may be very muddy in the wet season (unless it's been rebuilt).  In a half-mile the trail climbs moderately through a pleasant forest of fir and cedar and passes beneath a giant rotten log called the "fallen tree arch."  Look for a rare seven-foot diameter old-growth douglas fir tree nearby. Beyond, the trail descends to another junction; stay right to continue the hike, or left to reach the lower lake trail.  Go right

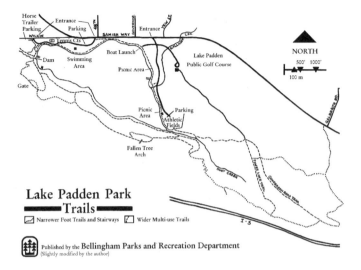

Lake Padden Park
**Trails**

Narrower Foot Trails and Stairways    Wider Multi-use Trails

Published by the Bellingham Parks and Recreation Department
(Slightly modified by the author)

at the next junction and begin a series of meanders and short steep switchbacks up to the ridge crest. The trail improves and an uncommon view of I-5 and the Chuckanut Mountain area is reached about a mile from the last cut-off to the lake. Pass beneath powerlines into forest then back along the powerlines to the edge of the golf course. Bend sharply to the left to return to Lake Padden (a right turn leads to more trails and a trailhead on Samish Way near Galbraith Rd.). This final leg of the hike descends gently through maturing forest, rotting stumps and verdant wetlands to the obvious trail along the lakeshore and the return to the starting point.

# 18. Fragrance Lake

*Hiking distance: 2 - 5 miles RT*       *Time: Allow 2 - 4 hours*
*Elevation gain: 1000 - 1800 feet*     *Season: Year-round*

A favorite year-round hike for many locals, the Fragrance Lake trail passes through deep forest on the way to a nice loop around the lake. Years ago, an earthen dam was built to raise the lake level, but it weakened in a storm, gave way and sent a wall of water raging down the mountain. Several homes were destroyed in the vicinity of today's Chuckanut Fire Station, and the Interurban trolley which just happened to be passing by was badly damaged.

There are three approaches to the lake (*maps, p. 56 & 140*). The most popular begins at the west trailhead on Chuckanut Dr. near the main entrance to Larrabee State Park, 5 miles south of Fairhaven (well signed). Another, the north access, begins 0.7 mile up the Cleator Rd. just before a gate. The third begins about 2.5 miles up the same road. One can also combine the Fragrance Lake hike with a visit to Chuckanut Ridge (*hike #19*) or Lost Lake (*hike #20*). Eventually, a new barrier-free trail along "Fragrance Ridge" (*see map*) will be constructed along old logging grades and through a tiny patch of old-growth forest. This and other planned links in the Chuckanuts promise an outstanding network of trails for all nonmotorized users.

Beginning at Chuckanut Dr. across from the north entrance to the State Park, hike up a short way to the Interurban Trail, cross and follow the gently ascending route about 0.9 mile to

Trillium

a junction. A left takes you 0.2 mile to a good viewpoint of Georgia Strait and the islands. At the junction, stay right another mile on a gradually steepening path, cross a small stream and reach another junction near a gravel road and former parking area 0.2 mile before the lake. (The old road to Fragrance Lake was closed to motor vehicles several years ago and may not reopen.) The lake trail (left) drops down slightly to another junction. Go left or straight to complete the easy loop around the lake.

The north approach climbs steadily, passes a small waterfall and reaches the lake near its outlet. Avoiding cliffs, stay left at the ridge crest, descend slightly, and ramble upstream to find the loop trail nearby. Or, follow the trail along the ridge for a good view of the lake (high cliffs: use caution). The east approach is the shortest but less interesting. The path off Cleator Rd. is well marked and follows an old logging road that descends gently to the old parking area above to the loop trail around the lake. This east route is popular among horses and mountain bikes.

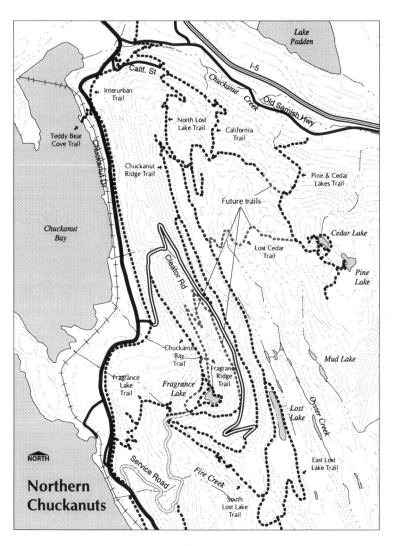

Lake Padden

Calif. St

Chuckanut Creek

I-5

Old Samish Hwy

Interurban Trail

North Lost Lake Trail

California Trail

Teddy Bear Cove Trail

Chuckanut Dr.

Chuckanut Ridge Trail

Pine & Cedar Lakes Trail

Chuckanut Bay

Future trails

Cedar Lake

Cleator Rd

Lost Cedar Trail

Pine Lake

Chuckanut Bay Trail

Fragrance Ridge Trail

Mud Lake

Fragrance Lake Trail

Fragrance Lake

Lost Lake

Oyster Creek

NORTH

Service Road

Fire Creek

East Lost Lake Trail

**Northern Chuckanuts**

South Lost Lake Trail

# 19. Chuckanut Ridge

*Hiking distance: 1 - 9 miles RT*    *Time: Allow 1 - 6 hours*
*Elevation gain: 0 - 400 feet*       *Season: Year-round*

With the recent acquisition of land along Chuckanut Ridge by county and state park agencies (thanks in part to Trillium Corporation), this exceptional hike is now one of the best in the lowlands. The trail is rough and passes very close to cliffs, so due caution is in order. The trail can be approached from the west or south off Cleator Rd. and from the north by way of Lost Lake trail (*hike #20*). The ridge trail is likely to be improved soon, along with several new links to other trails in the vicinity (*maps, p. 56 & 140*).

To reach the west or south trailhead, take Chuckanut Dr. four miles south of Fairhaven to High Line Rd. which quickly becomes the Cleator Rd. Follow the latter 2.5 miles to Middle Ridge Trail, the easier approach (trail is hidden on the left; good viewpoint 0.5 mile up), or 3.5 miles to Cyrus Gates Overlook; walk a short distance back down the road (or new trail) to the trail at the first road switchback. In less than 100 yards, find a good view of Mt. Baker and Lost Lake, a stone's throw away but 600 feet below. The 300-foot cliffs of Oyster Dome (*hike #22*) are visible to the southeast three miles distant. Continue northward, generally near the ridgetop, eventually passing a junction with Middle Ridge Trail. You will find ups and downs, good trail and some rough trail with excellent views to the east: Mt. Baker, Lookout Mt. and Lake Padden, and meager views to west: Georgia Strait, Chuckanut Bay, and Lummi Island. The ridge becomes skinnier and more

*Four-legged best friends have a distinct advantage on Chuckanut Ridge.*

dramatic two miles from the start, offering increasingly pleasant spots to sit and soak in the sandstone scenery.

Eventually, the trail descends to a large clearing (good views) and a residential subdivision high on the ridge. About 1/4 mile before this clearing, a rough spur trail to the right (east) winds down through sandstone and forest to a junction with the Lost Lake Trail. Go left to reach California St. and Arroyo Park. A right takes you to Lost Lake (in two miles) and a long loop option back to the south end of Chuckanut Ridge. From the Lost Lake Trail just above the gate near Fragrance Lake Road (2.5 miles beyond Lost Lake) climb the ridge trail a short mile to the upper parking lot. (*see hike #20*).

# 20. Lost Lake

*Hiking distance: 5.5 - 11 miles RT*  *Time: Allow 4 - 8 hours*
*Elevation gain: 1000 feet*  *Season: Year-round*

The lands surrounding Lost Lake are a recent addition to
Larrabee State Park, vastly improving future prospects for a
well linked trail system on Chuckanut Mountain. Eventually,
new sections of trail may connect the park with Pine and
Cedar Lakes and Samish Park to the east. While most hikers
follow old logging roads to and from Lost Lake, loop and side
trips are described for enjoying a little more of the Chuckanut
wilderness. The usual approach is from the southwest via
Fragrance Lake Trail (*hike #18*). However, the northern
approach from Arroyo Park/ California St. is getting popular
and is also described (*maps, p. 56 & 140*).

*Southwest approach:* From the trail junction next to the old
parking area at Fragrance Lake (just above the loop trail
around the lake), walk down the Fragrance Lake Rd. 200
yards. Turn left on an old logging road with a white gate—the
official Lost Lake trailhead. Walk this old road with partial
winter views of Samish Bay and the San Juan Islands to a
saddle at 1.4 mile (450 foot gain to here); stay left. Note the
path to the right is the optional return route. From the saddle,
it's another 1.1 miles and a 400' descent to the lake and a
junction at its north end; make a sharp right to reach the lake
(going straight takes you to California St., three miles distant.)
A 0.2 mile walk through a dense damp tunnel of vegetation
brings you to the soggy lake shore. At a small clearing, follow
the trail up a short bank and south along the narrow rocky

ridge rimming the lake's east shore to good views and rest stops. The rock can be slick where it hugs the edge of small cliffs. The outlet stream flows across rocky slabs disappearing over a waterfall into the forest below (slippery; be cautious).

For the loop, continue along the low ridge past clearcuts and 0.3 mile past the south end of the lake to an old road bed. In another 0.3 mile, turn right on a path just before the old road bed starts to curve to the left (goes to Bloedel timber lands and logging roads to Lake Samish). Follow the path a winding mile through quiet forest, regaining 400' of elevation; stay right at trail junctions; or go left to explore older forest and more views in a half-mile. The way curves north to the saddle where you rejoin the main trail. Take care not to lose your bearing; the dense forest can be disorienting.

*North approach:* To reach Lost Lake from the north, begin at Arroyo Park, crossing Chuckanut Creek on a bridge. After a short climb beyond the bridge, grab an obvious trail on the left contouring up through forest and a few mud holes to California St., an unpaved former logging road. Turn left on this road and right at a road junction nearby. Stay on this old road all the way to Lost Lake, about four miles to the south. Well before the lake, just beyond a short set of switchbacks, look for the spur trail to Chuckanut Ridge on the right near a tiny stream. The hike to the top and a short jaunt north or south make this a worthwhile side trip.

# 21. Pine & Cedar Lakes

*Hiking distance: 4 - 6 miles RT*    *Time: Allow 2.5 - 5 hours*
*Elevation gain: 1300 - 1600 feet*    *Season: Year-round*

Two very pleasant lakes and views of the San Juan Islands and
Mt. Rainier on a clear day make this a rewarding hike almost
any time. Cedar Lake has a loop trail around it and Pine Lake
has a small island-peninsula with campsites nearby.
Eventually, an improved trail system may connect this area
with Lost Lake, Larrabee State Park, and Lake Samish.

From Fairhaven (12th & Old Fairhaven Parkway), follow
Chuckanut Drive (SR 11) south 1.3 miles, turning left on Old
Samish Hwy. Continue another 1.9 miles to the signed
trailhead and parking area on the right (*map, p. 56*). The broad
path, an old logging road, is steep the first 1.5 miles, passes a
couple of dead-end spur trails and a sign in a tree. It finally
levels out before reaching the Cedar Lake junction. Keep
walking to reach Pine Lake, or turn left to lose 100 feet of
elevation in the few hundred yards down to Cedar Lake. Hike
either direction around the lake and watch for the spur trail
on the west end leading up to several viewpoints 1/4 to 1/2
mile away. The first (to the right) looks toward Bellingham,
the second, up the ridge a little farther, looks toward the
Cascades and Pine Lake. Here, the path becomes harder to
follow in the dense thicket of young trees, but the third
viewpoint is close by and overlooks the San Juan Islands.

At the lakes junction, the main trail leads 1/2 mile to the
scenic, less visited Pine Lake. Approach quietly to avoid

scaring off ducks and other native wildlife. No trail circles this
lake, but the island-peninsula near the west edge is a fine spot to
lay out the picnic cloth. Several campsites exist near the shore and
fishing is permitted in season at both lakes. Allow four hours to
hike the entire route.

## Raptor Ridge

*Trail volunteers, Raptor Ridge overlook.*

Back where the trail lev-
eled out—before you
reached the Cedar Lake
turn-off (about 1.5 mile
from the trailhead)—is a
junction with the Hem-
lock Trail. This level grade
is a remnant of the rail-
road logging era of the
1920s and the Hemlock
follows it for 0.3 mile before dipping down, rounding a bend and
climbing slightly to a junction with the new Raptor Ridge Trail,
0.6 mile from the Pine and Cedar Trail. (Hemlock Trail continues
three miles to Arroyo Park in Bellingham). In 1999, the author
along with forty volunteers from the Bellingham Mountaineers,
Sierra Club and others constructed the 0.4-mile footpath to Raptor Ridge—a name given to the wooded ridge and high cliff band
at the end of this scenic, moderately steep, wildlife-sensitive trail.
Hawks, eagles, owls, ravens and turkey vultures are often seen or
heard, so amble quietly across small bridges, up a stone staircase
(watch your head!), past rocky outcrops and grottos to a
panoramic view of the Oyster Creek watershed—the wild heart
of the Chuckanuts. Use caution at the overlook. It slopes off to a
very long drop (maybe constrain the kids and pets first time up).
Be extra cautious in strong wind or when snowy or icy.

# 22. Oyster Dome & S. Chuckanut Mt.

*Distance: 5 - 6 miles RT*  
*Elevation gain: 1600 - 2000 feet*

*Time: Allow 3 - 5 hours*  
*Season: Almost year-round*

There are several approaches to the South Chuckanut (Blanchard Mt.) area, with access to Oyster Dome, the so-called "bat caves," Lily and Lizard Lakes, and other destinations. (*For the east approach see hike #23.*) Among the rewards are talus caves and outstanding views of Bellingham and Samish Bays, Georgia Strait, the San Juan and Gulf Islands, Skagit Valley, and the North Cascade and Olympic Mountains. The caves, which are really just large crevices in a giant boulder field, require spelunking skills to be explored. (Avoid them fall through spring to protect a highly sensitive species of bats.) For this hike, the boulder field and a

*Zuh view from zuh top.*

spectacular viewpoint high above are the recommended destinations (*maps, p. 66 & 140*).

From Fairhaven, follow Chuckanut Dr. (SR 11) ten miles to a turn-out a mile past the hairpin bridge at Oyster Creek. Across the road the marked trail climbs steeply through maturing second-growth forest. The path soon enters a large clearcut (at least the views are good) and keeps climbing below a hang-glider launch at the ridgetop called Samish Overlook. The trail works left not so steeply and reenters the forest. At a junction a sharp right goes 0.5 mile to the Overlook and great views. Stay left to continue. Cross a couple of small streams and go right at a junction with the original "bat caves" trail. (A left leads down about 1.5 mile to an unpaved, possibly restricted private road and Chuckanut Dr. just north of your starting point.) Stay right, climbing more steeply past a small cascade and two large rock outcrops on the left. In 1/4 mile more watch for a signed spur trail to the left leading 150 yards to the boulder field. The high cliffs of Oyster Dome lean out precariously over an unusual landscape of house-sized boulders. Explore this broad heaping pile of rubble with care. Wet or moss-covered rocks offer poor footing, and deep holes and crevices, some hidden beneath thick vegetation, threaten to swallow those with shorter attention spans. For the final steep push to the top, return to the main trail and head uphill 0.3 mile to a junction. Lily Lake is an easy mile to the right. Go left 0.4 mile to find the top of Oyster Dome and the best view in the Chuckanuts. Mt. Rainier is visible on the clearest days. The area may be dangerous to rambunctious young'ns, or to the rest of us if snowy, icy or windy.

# 23. Lily & Lizard Lakes

*Distance: 8 - 11 miles RT*  *Time: Allow 4 - 8 hours*
*Elevation gain: 1000 - 2000 feet*  *Season: Almost year-round*

Two quiet lakes in a heavily forested setting are the reward for this moderate hike up the east flank of Blanchard Mountain. The trail is also the eastern approach for Oyster Dome (*see hike #22*). From I-5, take the Alger exit (#240), go west 0.4 mile and turn left on Barrel Springs Rd. In another 0.7 mile, turn right on a good gravel logging road (trail sign). The upper Lily and Lizard Lakes trailhead and parking area (a few yards beyond) are reached in less than two miles, just past a spur road to the left which goes to Samish Overlook.

*Early morning view of Mt. Baker near the Lily & Lizard Lakes trailhead.*

The way to the lakes junction (Lily left, Lizard right) is well marked and easy to follow. Many of the trails in this area follow old logging railroad grades, as evidenced by a few ties and an occasional steel rail. It is about three miles to Lily Lake and four to Lizard Lake, with a total gain of 1,500 feet. There are campsites at both lakes. When you reach Lily Lake, a less obvious path leaves the north end of the lake and climbs up to a rock outcrop and a good viewpoint about 0.4 mile away. Back at the main trail, head west 1.5 mile to access Oyster Dome. Another slightly shorter approach to Oyster Dome (*see hike #22*) is by way of the road to Samish Overlook. The signed trailhead is located on a landing just below the first hang-glider launch. A major new 6-mile trail from Lizard Lake to Lost Lake ("Lost Lizard Trail") is in the planning stages.

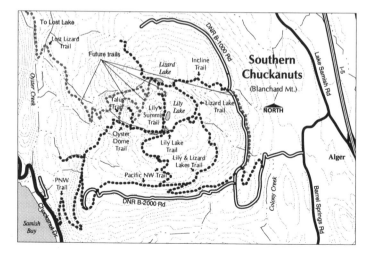

# 24. Lake Whatcom Trail

*Distance: 2 - 6 miles RT*                    *Time: Allow 1 - 3 hours*
*Elevation gain: None*                        *Season: Year-round*

The second-best part of this walk is a small but scenic waterfall
encountered less than a mile from the start. The best part is
the fact that you are rarely more than a few feet from the lake
almost the entire way. The route generally follows an old
railroad grade that once connected Bellingham sawmills with
the timber brought down from the Lake Whatcom and South
Fork Nooksack watersheds. The trailhead is near the site of a
proposed county park on Smith Creek. There are exceptional
opportunities here for a future trail network connecting the
lake shore with small stands of ancient trees, high rocky bluffs
and viewpoints, and impressive gorges and waterfalls.

Follow North Shore Drive around the north end of Lake
Whatcom past Agate Bay, and across the new bridge at Smith
Creek. Park at the well marked trailhead just beyond (8 miles
from Bloedel-Donovan Park). Walk around the gate and
follow the trail through a pleasant forest of cedar and maple.
Reach the old Blue Canyon railroad grade in 1/4 mile. The
waterfall framed in mossy rock walls appears about 20
minutes from the start. Beyond, steep rock cliffs and several
giant douglas fir trees, some in excess of six feet in diameter,
loom high above. These are mixed with cedar, maple and
interestingly, madrone trees which are more common to
west-facing saltwater bluffs. Cross two more streams on the
walk toward Blue Canyon Rd.

In two miles, find a pleasant park-like spot on the right for a lunch or swim break. This is also a good turn-around point. The trail continues another mile but ends abruptly at a fence. The County is working to secure access to the last few hundred feet of abandoned railroad grade to make the connection to the South Bay area, a critical hiking and bicycling link on Lake Whatcom.

*Rare old-growth douglas fir just off the Lake Whatcom Trail.*

# 25. Tennant Lk/Hovander Homestead

*Distance: 1.5 - 4 miles RT*          *Time: Allow 1 - 3 hours*
*Elevation Gain: 50 feet*             *Season: Year-round*

This walk combines two viewing towers, a boardwalk
through the marsh, a fragrance garden, interpretive center,
game reserve, and an historic farmstead on two attractive
adjoining parks totalling nearly 350 acres. There is good
birding here in winter and spring, and hunting which tends
to keep the boardwalk closed a few too many days each year.
From I-5 exit #262, head west 0.5 mile, turning left on
Hovander Rd. immediately past a railroad overpass. Fork

*Tennant Lake view tower.*

right on Nielsen Rd. (signs) to reach Tennant Lake Interpretive Center and the parking area.

Begin the walk at the view tower (bring binoculars), take the path over a bridge to the boardwalk–a viewpoint is 50 yards to the left. Stay right to begin a long loop that weaves an interesting course through shadowy swamp. Move quietly to see perching and aquatic birds and maybe a muskrat. Listen for the metallic whistles of red-winged blackbirds and the high pitched trills of the elusive winter wren. Back at the parking lot, a signed path goes 0.5 mile west to Hovander Homestead (a ten minute walk). Visit turn of the century farm buildings, another view tower, the old farmhouse full of antiques, and gardens and picnic areas. The river is close by and offers a bit of exploring as well. For an extended walk, follow the gravel road south from the Tennant Lake parking lot to a dike (beware of hunters in season). Head left to reach Slater Rd. in one mile. Watch for beavers, eagles, acrobatic swallows, lone woodpeckers and happy warblers flitting in the brush.

# 26. South Fork Nooksack River

*Distance: 1 - 6 miles RT*       *Time: Allow 1 - 4 hours*
*Elevation gain: 200 feet*       *Season: Year-round*

Except for the mud holes near the start, the South Fork "trail" offers an enjoyable walk along the river. Late summer or early fall is the best time to visit, although cold clear winter days when the ground is frozen are also nice. When there's snow, the route make's a good cross-country ski tour. The people of Whatcom County recently had the good fortune of securing several hundred acres along the South Fork Nooksack, largely through donations from the Syre and Nesset families, which will add tremendously to the public's ability to enjoy and preserve the natural values and rural historic character of the area for generations to come.

From Highway 9, two miles south of Acme, drive east on the Saxon Road 3.5 miles to its end near the Skookum Creek Fish Hatchery. Park across the bridge and begin walking southward along the old road closest to the river. In 0.5 mile, a long stretch of large mud holes may require minor detours through woods to avoid wet feet. Overgrown side roads and paths provide access to beaver ponds and gravel bars. Edfro Creek is crossed in a mile and Cavanaugh Creek at 2.3 miles, just before the old site of Dyes' Ranch. The area is rich in marsh habitat and wildlife. Between the two creeks, the river flows through a narrow rocky gorge once considered a possible dam site. The old road can be followed into Skagit County where it emerges into an area of huge clearcuts.

# 27. Racehorse Falls

*Distance: 1 mile RT*              *Time: Allow 1 hour or less*
*Elevation gain: 100 feet*         *Season: Year-round*

This is a short, rough walk along the creek through an attractive vine maple and cedar forest.  From Mt. Baker Highway, turn right on the Mosquito Lake Road (MP 16.8), then left in a mile on the North Fork Road.  Watch for bald eagles along the river in winter.  Turn right in 4.1 miles (just before the creek) and park at a road bend in 0.1 mile.  The slightly hidden trail is on the left.  Follow it through quiet forest to a flood channel; stay right.  Ten yards before the creek, a rough path goes right and hugs the steep hillside.  A few logs are crossed before the falls come into view.  Clamber over rocks to a tiny beach just below the falls.

A slightly better view is had from the top of an obvious rock ramp, although it may be slippery and hazardous when wet or icy; stay right.  Avoid it altogether if unsure.  The noisy waterfall is not huge but the setting is unique and well worth the effort.  Below the falls, Racehorse Creek is an important salmon stream.

*Racehorse Falls.*

# Mt. Baker Area

# 28. Horseshoe Bend

*Distance: 0.5 - 5 miles RT*      *Time: Allow 1 - 3 hours*
*Elevation gain: 200 feet*      *Season: Year-round*

A nice hike even on a crummy day, this easy trip is suitable
for families almost any time of year. The trail winds along the
North Fork Nooksack River at the edge of a deep forest. A
rushing tumult of melting snow and glaciers, the river seems
to be building momentum here for the hard push across the
lowlands to Bellingham Bay. The reach is popular with
kayakers who slalom through rapids near the SR 542 bridge.

Park at the trailhead on Mt. Baker Hwy (MP 35.4) across from
the Douglas Fir Campground, 2 miles east of the Glacier
Public Service Center. The trail begins at the bridge and
meanders upriver along noisy whitewater crashing over
boulders and bedrock. Sword ferns and moss form a thick
carpet beneath a dense second-growth forest of red cedar,
douglas fir, hemlock, vine maple and red alder. In early
summer trillium, wild ginger, bunchberry, twin flower and
Indian pipe share the damp forest floor with devil's club,
salmonberry and other shades of green.

In 1/4 mile cross Coal Creek and continue to the namesake
bend in the river a mile beyond. Just around the bend turn
right on an old road. In 100 yards the trail goes right another
mile and a half and ends at a point where it disappears over
the edge of a large washout. There are no great views of
surrounding peaks, but the rushing water, especially in
spring, makes it one of the best river walks in the county.

# 29. Church Mountain

*Distance:* *9 miles RT*          *Time:* *Allow 5 - 6 hours*
*Elevation gain:* *4,100 feet*     *Season:* *July - October*

Church Mt., named for the rock "steeple" at its summit, is very prominent from Mt. Baker Hwy about a mile east of the Glacier Public Service Center. It is a fairly strenuous climb with the trail gaining about 1,000' per mile on the way up to the old lookout site. Although the building has been gone for 25 years, its location on Church Mt. was strategic to fire control in the Nooksack watershed. This lovely rocky ridge is the western extremity of the High Divide, a ten mile ridge system of uninterrupted meadows reaching all the way to Yellow Aster Meadows above Swamp Creek (*see hikes #31 & 34*).

Turn left off Mt. Baker Highway (MP 38.7) just beyond Fossil Creek onto Road #3040. In about 2 miles, the road crosses the creek bed (park here if not driveable). The trailhead is 1/2 mile beyond at the road end (elevation 2,000'). The trail follows the old logging road initially, then enters a shadowy wilderness for the long ascent to the meadows and first good views at 3 miles. After contouring westward another 0.5 mile, the trail switchbacks up the final wildflower slopes toward the rocky point above. The final few steps are literally carved out of the rock face. The top, a flat rocky veranda at 6,100

feet, makes a fine munching place. Soaking up the views... Mt. Baker, the Nooksack Valley, Mt. Shuksan and countless distant peaks on both sides of the international border. Close by to the west is the summit of Church Mt. with its near vertical walls. Experienced cross-country hikers may find a way down to the north 500 feet to Kidney Lakes and Whistler Lakes (*see hike #30*), or work up to the small saddle west of point 5,580' to wander east along the High Divide toward Excelsior Pass (good campsites either way). By mid-summer, carry extra water, since the high ridge is very dry, especially on the south side.

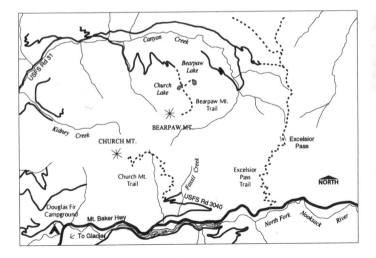

# 30.  Church Lake & Bearpaw Mt.

*Distance:  2.5 - 11 miles RT*          *Time:  Allow 2 - 7 hours*
*Elevation gain:  500 - 3,000 feet*     *Season:  Mid-July - October*

At the west end of the High Divide, alpine lakes and meadows between Church Mt. and Bearpaw Mt. comprise a seldom visited wilderness, contrasting sharply with massive logging scars that characterize much of the Canyon Creek valley. Clearcutting has occurred at very high elevations (near 5,000′); an uneasy benefit, however, is better access to Church Lake and the extensive meadows surrounding Bearpaw Mt. Strangely, this portion of the Divide was not included in the 1984 Washington Wilderness Act which designated lands to the east as part of the Mt. Baker Wilderness.

The primary access, Canyon Creek Rd., was heavily damaged at MP 7 and beyond by floods in the winter of 1989-90 but was recently reopened all the way to the Damfino Lakes/Excelsior Pass Trailhead.  The old campground on Canyon Creek was destroyed.  Drive 2 miles east of Glacier on Mt. Baker Highway, turning left (MP 35.6) on Canyon Creek Road #31 (*map, p. 77*).  Follow this narrow paved road about 10 miles, then turn right on Road #3160, just past the old Canyon Creek Campground. (This road may be rough, if passable at all.) Stay right at the first junction and left at the second.  The road ends at a saddle at the upper edge of the clearcut (about 4.5 miles from Canyon Creek Road).

The approach may be difficult, but the hike certainly isn't.  The unmarked trail continues to the right (south) through open

*Camp robbers plotting a surprise lunchtime raid.*

forest, gradually ascending into subalpine country. The high cliffs of Bearpaw's north peak loom above an azure Church Lake which is about 0.7 mile from the trailhead. The path becomes less obvious as it climbs the long curving ridge that begins southeast of the lake and rises to the high meadow which is Bearpaw's true summit (6,062'). One could also climb the open meadows staying well to the left of the cliffs. From the summit, the High Divide, Mt. Baker and Mt. Shuksan are spectacular. More experienced hikers with good map and compass skills may descend to the southwest to discover a number of small lakes and wild meadows leading to Whistler Lakes and Church Mt. in the distance. There are many good campsites (but go easy on the vegetation).

# 31. Excelsior Pass & High Divide

*Distance: 5 - 8 miles RT*　　　　*Time: Allow 3 - 6 hours*
*Elevation gain: 1,200 - 3,500 feet*　*Season: July - October*

There are two approaches to this extensive alpine ridge, the northerly one via Damfino Lakes being a tad easier to hike given 2,500 feet less elevation gain (*map, p. 77*). Both lead to exceptional meadows and good views of Mt. Baker, the North Cascades, and peaks of the British Columbia Coast Range. From Excelsior Pass, one can wander this heather and wildflower ridge for miles in either direction. Since there are at least five trails which access the High Divide, numerous day hikes and overnight trips are possible.

The south trailhead is on the Mt. Baker Highway (MP 41) 8 miles east of the Glacier Public Service Center. This steep wooded trail climbs 3,500' in 4 miles to the pass. Most of the route is in heavy forest, breaking out into meadows the last mile. To reach the shorter northern start, turn left on Canyon Creek Rd #31 (MP 35.6) and drive this 13.5 miles to a fork. Stay left and reach the trailhead 1.5 miles farther. The trail meets a junction with the Boundary Way Trail in 0.7 mile (leads north up Canyon Ridge) just before Damfino Lakes - stay right. The muddy trail is easy to follow and gently climbs to drier meadows after 2 miles, reaching the 5,300' pass in 2.5 miles. From here, one can hike up several hundred feet to higher viewpoints in either direction. The old Excelsior Lookout site is 0.2 mile to the east and 400' above. Mt. Baker, Chowder Ridge and the heavily crevassed Roosevelt Glacier are prominent to the south, as is Mt. Shuksan to the southeast.

If you're good with a map, it's feasible to ramble westward near the ridge top for several miles toward Church Mt., or eastward on the High Divide Trail to Welcome Pass, five miles from Excelsior Pass (*see hike #34*). Carry extra water. Snow is usually gone and wildflowers are at their peak by late July.

# 32. Mount Baker Trail

*Distance: 6 - 8 miles RT*　　　*Time: Allow 4 - 6 hours*
*Elevation gain: 1,400 - 2,300 feet*　*Season: July - October*

Also called Heliotrope Ridge Trail, this popular route for hikers and climbers alike offers one of the best places to get up close and personal with a river of ice, namely, the Coleman Glacier. For just a moderate effort, the scenic rewards are plenty: ancient forest, wildflowers, mountain streams and waterfalls, the Coleman and Roosevelt Glaciers, Mt. Baker, and the Black Buttes.

*Climbers at the glacier's edge.*

From Mt. Baker Highway, a mile past the town of Glacier, turn right (south) on the Glacier Creek Rd #39. Follow this narrow winding road almost eight miles to the obvious trailhead on the left. The trail gradually climbs through open forest to a series of switchbacks and waterfall views before passing the site of the old Kulshan Cabin about 2 miles up. Just beyond, the path leaves the forest where views quickly improve. Stay left at a junction for the easy stroll (some stream hopping) to the brink of a lateral moraine overlooking the Coleman Glacier. The edge is loose and sloughing away so be cautious, and by all means stay off the glacier (unless you're an experienced climber with a rope team, ice axes, crampons and the like).

Beaten paths up the moraine and through rocky meadows offer more exploring. Or, return to the junction and hike up the "hogsback," the climbers' route up the mountain. Snow and ice blocks the way for hikers at about 6,000 feet. The Heliotrope Ridge crest is a half-mile to the west. Beware of high water, steep snow (with drop-offs below), thin snow bridges and avalanches in late spring - early summer.

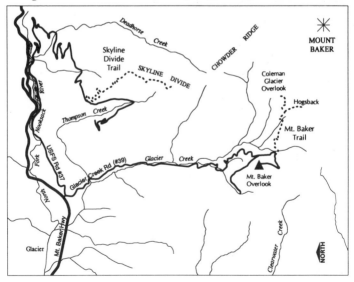

# 33. Cougar Divide

*Distance: 7 miles RT*  
*Elevation gain: 1,000 feet*  

*Time: Allow 4 - 6 hours*  
*Season: Mid-July - October*

This pleasant trail is not easy to get to, but it does provide a comparable, less populated alternative to the heavily used Skyline Divide Trail to the west (the latter is well described in other guidebooks). The trailhead is high (4,800') and the views are good much of the way. It's a very long bumpy drive to the trailhead, though most small cars should do okay if the road has been recently graded. From Mt. Baker Highway (MP 40.7), turn right on the Wells Creek Road #33 and continue across the bridge beyond Nooksack Falls (*viewpoint #16*). At a road junction, make a hard right and follow this up the Wells Creek valley to a bridge at Mile 6 and a view of Mt. Baker and the Hadley Glacier. From here it's another 6 miles and 2,000 feet up a winding rough road to another junction; stay left. Just beyond, follow a right fork a short distance to the possibly unmarked trailhead on the left.

The trail is not regularly maintained but is in fair condition as it gently climbs southward through old snags in a miniature subalpine forest. A high knoll (5,382') is reached in 3/4 mile, offering a suitable turn-around point for a short walk. The path meanders through unusual volcanic terrain to a point where the ridge

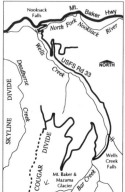

*Chowder Ridge and Mt. Baker.*

drops down to a wooded area. Watch for the trail down to your left. For the next mile the path is generally good and stays close to the ridge crest in thick forest. At several points a short steep slippery section or fallen log may be discouraging but are quite passable.

After a small pond, a meadow is crossed on a side slope before gaining the crest again. From here the views of Mt. Shuksan, Mt. Baker, Hadley Peak and Chowder Ridge are scenic and impressive. The trail ends where Cougar Divide intersects rugged Chowder Ridge in colorful and fragile (often soggy) meadows 3.5 miles from the start. Camping is not recommended. Stay on the trail and don't build any fires. More experienced hikers can wander up to the southwest through rock and snow to more views at the ridge crest.

# 34. Welcome Pass

*Distance: 5 - 7 miles RT*          *Time: Allow 4 - 6 hours*
*Elevation gain: 3,000 - 3,700 feet*      *Season: Mid-July - October*

One of several access routes to the High Divide, the Welcome
Pass Trail may be the toughest. As always, the views help ease
the pain of getting there. The trailhead is at the end of Road
#3060 just west of Silver Fir Campground. Turn left off the
Mt. Baker Highway at MP 45.8 and drive 0.8 mile to the
trailhead and parking area just beyond (*map, p. 88*). If
undriveable, park in the highway turn-out nearby and walk
the road.

Endless short switchbacks (67 of them) go almost from
trailhead to summit. Expect to gain 2,400 feet in barely two
miles, making Welcome Pass one of the steepest hikes in the
North Cascades. Lower down there are enticing views of Mt.
Shuksan across the North Fork Nooksack River, and Mt. Baker
through small breaks in the trees. If you've been counting
switchbacks, the crest will be very close by the time you round
#67. The trail empties into open meadows and views of most
major peaks in the region with Tomyhoi Peak cutting the
clouds to the north. If that isn't enough, wander west a mile
on the High Divide Trail, climbing another 600 to 700 feet of
ridge for the big 360º view. Mt. Baker, of course, looms, rises,
juts, sticks out, and/or hovers to the SSW, always a
spectacular sight. British Columbia lies just eight million
millimeters to the north.

# 35. Winchester Mountain

*Distance: 4 - 7 miles RT*  *Time: Allow 3 - 5 hours*
*Elevation gain: 1,300 - 2,400 feet*  *Season: Mid-July - October*

The lookout atop Winchester Mountain is an impressive vantage point that offers sprawling views of major peaks, lakes and the high country north of Mt. Baker. By the time the snow has melted away (maybe by mid-July), it is a popular place, especially on fair summer weekends. To avoid crowds, plan your visit on a weekday or wait until fall.

To reach the trailhead, turn left on the Twin Lakes Rd. #3065 off Mt. Baker Highway at MP 46.2, 12.7 miles east of the Glacier Public Service Center (*map, p. 88*). At a junction, stay left and continue about 5 miles to a parking area at the Gold Run Pass/Tomyhoi Lake Trailhead. The road is often washed out beyond this point, so walk (or drive?) the remaining 1.5 or 2 miles to Twin Lakes (elevation 5,200'). These high lakes can be snow covered into July. The trail goes between them, contouring the southeast slope of Winchester a short distance to a junction with the High Pass/Gargett Mine Trail (*see hike #36*); turn left. The trail climbs moderately through scenic sloping meadows and occasional steep rocky sections. Near the ridge crest, lingering snow in early summer requires an ice axe (and the ability to use it) due to steep snow and dangerous cliffs below; don't hesitate to turn back if conditions warrant.

About 1.5 mile from the lakes, the ridge is met at 6,000 feet where views improve significantly. The final short switchbacks lead up the southwest side of the mountain to the restored lookout cabin at the summit. The views are *tremendo*: clockwise from north, Canadian and American Border Peaks, Mt. Larrabee, Goat Mt., Mt. Shuksan, Mt. Baker, the Nooksack River valley, Tomyhoi Peak and Tomyhoi Lake. The cozy, nicely windowed lookout is maintained by volunteers of the Mt. Baker Hiking Club (see the list of organizations at the end of the book). Without their efforts, the building may have disappeared by now, as is the case with most of the old fire lookouts of the North Cascades.

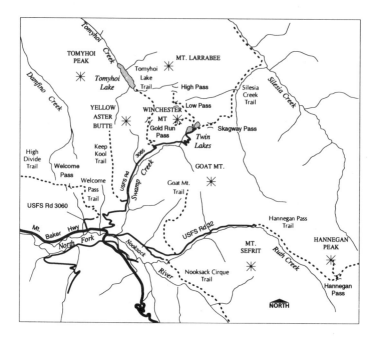

*Winchester Mountain from Twin Lakes, still icy in July.*

*Tomyhoi Peak and Lake from High Pass.*

# 36. High Pass & Gargett Mine

*Distance: 3 - 8 miles RT*  *Time: Allow 2 - 6 hours*
*Elevation gain: 700 - 1,900 feet*  *Season: Mid-July - October*

The abandoned mine on the southern flank of Mt. Larrabee
has collapsed, but a few old relics and continuous views make
it a good destination for an easy day trip. The greater
elevation applies if the road to Twin Lakes is not driveable.
(Refer to hike #35, Winchester Mt., for directions to the
trailhead at Twin Lakes; *map, p. 88.*) At the junction above
Twin Lakes, stay right (left goes up Winchester Mt.). Follow
the path over a shoulder, then traverse along the steep,
partially-wooded northeast slope. In 1 mile, a series of
switchbacks through wildflowers gain about 400 feet to Low
Pass. (For a possible loop trip around Winchester Mt.,
experienced cross-country hikers can descend to the
southwest to meadows and the Gold Run Pass-Tomyhoi Lake
Trail 1.3 miles away. Head left and over the pass back to the
Twin Lakes Rd. - about 7.5 miles total.)

From Low Pass the trail climbs the subalpine ridge crest and
skirts a high knoll, reaching High Pass (elev. 6,000') 2.5 miles
from the lakes. The Gargett brothers' mine and remnants are
visible to the north about 250 feet below. Tomyhoi Lake
shines against the 2,500 foot high cliffs of Tomyhoi Peak.
Continue along a less used path to the east for a closer view
of the precipitous Pleiades ridge east of Mt. Larrabee. The
lookout can also be seen atop Winchester Mt. A combined trip
to High Pass and Winchester Lookout requires a full day, but
it's not an unreasonable outing for ambitious types.

# 37. Hannegan Pass & Peak

*Distance: 8 - 10 miles RT*     *Time: Allow 5 - 7 hours*
*Elevation gain: 2,000 - 3,000 feet*     *Season: July - October*

Hannegan Pass is a popular hike and is the nearest access to the North Cascades National Park from Bellingham. The Park boundary is 5 miles from the trailhead just beyond the pass. (Consult the Park Service or guidebooks listed in the Introduction for backpacking possibilities: Whatcom Pass and Copper Ridge are major contenders.) Hannegan Pass is a good destination for a day hike, but a little extra effort takes you steeply up Hannegan Peak for another amazing panorama.

The trailhead is at the end of the Hannegan Road (#32), 5.5 miles from Mt. Baker Hwy. Turn left off the highway just before the Nooksack River bridge (MP 46.5) and stay left at a fork in 1.5 mile (*map, p. 88*). The trail is nearly flat the first mile, then slowly climbs through fragrant avalanche slopes and forest, crossing several small streams along the way (can be tricky in early summer). Views keep improving: south across Ruth Creek are the sheer rock walls of Nooksack Ridge and Mt. Sefrit; to the southeast, the solid white dome of Ruth Mt. at 7,106 feet above sea level. The trail steepens and switchbacks through subalpine meadows in the last mile before Hannegan Pass at 4 miles from the start. Allow 2 to 3 hours to reach the pass at 5,066 feet.

From the pass, a trail to the north (left) leads through woods to steep meadows and the summit of Hannegan Peak at 6,168 feet. As you clear timberline the big panorama emerges: Mt. Larrabee to the northwest, Mt. Sefrit to the west, Mt. Baker and Mt. Shuksan to the southwest, Ruth Mt. to the south, Mineral Mt., Mt. Challenger, the Picket Range and Glacier Peak (on the horizon) to the southeast, Copper Ridge to the east, Mt. Redoubt to the northeast and towering Slesse Mt. to the north, two miles inside Canada. From the pass, the main trail continues east, descending to the Chilliwack River (*hike #61*) and beyond to Whatcom Pass. An extended backpack over Whatcom Pass and down Big Beaver Valley to Ross Lake (a 40 mile trek) offers an exceptional excursion into the heart of the North Cascades.

*Ruth Mt. from Hannegan Peak.*

*Mt. Baker and Ptarmigan Ridge in winter.*

# 38. Ptarmigan Ridge

*Distance: 6.5 - 10 miles RT*　　*Time: Allow 4 - 7 hours*
*Elevation gain: 300 - 1,000 feet*　*Season: Mid-July- October*

The trailhead for Ptarmigan Ridge is located at Artist Point, one of the most scenic paved places anywhere in the Cascades Range. Drive 57.2 miles east from Bellingham (I-5) to the very end of Mt. Baker Hwy (usually snow-covered until July). From the southwest corner of this alpine parking lot, follow the Chain Lakes Trail across the south face of Table Mt. toward Mt. Baker (*map next page*). In 1.2 miles, a junction is reached; stay left for Ptarmigan Ridge; the right goes the short way to the lakes (*see hike #39*). The trail drops slightly and contours the broad ridge on its northwest side before crossing to the southeast in a mile. A small spur ridge is reached 0.9 mile farther: a good viewpoint and turn-around (3.1 miles and 400' gain to here). Even in August, hikers may encounter poor visibility and patches of snow over the trail, possibly requiring an ice axe (and the ability to use it). Snow, rain and wind can be serious hazards any time of year; turn back if conditions are crummy. There is no protection in case of bad weather (several trail travelers have met their maker here).

When free of snow (usually August-September), the upper portion of the ridge can be easily followed all the way to Coleman Pinnacle and the rocky meadows of Camp Kiser just beyond, about 4.5 miles from the trailhead. The entire trail is high and wild with great views of the Rainbow and Park Glaciers. Take care to keep your bearings, especially in deteriorating weather.

# 39. Bagley & Chain Lakes

*Distance:* 1.5 - 9 miles RT          *Time:* Allow 2 - 6 hours
*Elevation gain:* 200 - 2,000 feet     *Season:* July - October

Between Mt. Baker and Mt. Shuksan a major trail system offers easy to moderate walks and hikes and many loop possibilities from less than a mile to 20 miles or more. Easier walks include a 1.5 mile loop around lower Bagley Lake with a stop at the new Heather Meadows Visitor Center inside an historic building perched on a rocky overlook. The longer hike to Chain Lakes is extraordinary (and popular) summer and fall.

Drive Mt. Baker Hwy to the Mt. Baker Ski Area and turn right at the big map sign (MP 54.6) and right again in 0.1 mile to the parking lot. Follow signs to Bagley Lakes (right). The trail drops to the lower lake and heads for the dam at its outlet.

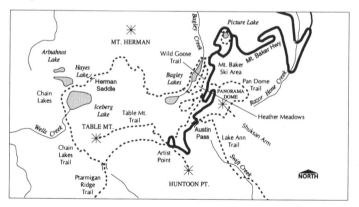

Turn left before crossing and wander a half-mile to the double-arch stone bridge. For an easy loop either go left uphill to the obvious visitor center and return via the Wild Goose Trail (*hike #40*), or cross the bridge and head back along the west side of the lower lake to the dam. To reach Chain Lakes cross the bridge and head southwest around the upper lake, climbing 1100 feet to Herman Saddle. Chain Lakes are 500 feet down the other side (4 miles to here). Mazama, Iceberg (the largest), Galena, and Hayes Lakes lie quiet in a magical setting. Turn back here, or for a more aggressive loop trip, continue 0.8 mile to a junction. (Left switchbacks up to a spectacular viewpoint 800 feet above the lakes.) Go straight 0.3 mile to Ptarmigan Ridge (*hike #38*). Walk left 1.2 mile to reach the parking lot at Artist Point, and left again to find the Wild Goose Trail (*hike #40*) for the 2 mile return to the start.

*Bagley Lakes stone bridge.*

# 40. Wild Goose Trail & Table Mt.

*Distance: 1.5 - 7 miles RT*          *Time: Allow 2 - 5 hours*
*Elevation gain: 300 - 1,700 feet*     *Season: July - October*

The new trail to Wild Goose Pass (aka Austin Pass) offers an aerobic alternative to driving all the way to Artist Point at the end of the Mt. Baker Hwy. (*See hike #39 for directions to the trailhead; map, p. 96.*) A 1.5 mile loop below Table Mt. to the Heather Meadows Visitor Center and back, and a 0.7 mile interpretive loop, the Fire and Ice Trail (beginning at the Center), offer two easy options. For the bigger workout follow the wild goose markers up from the visitor center (trail climbs below and parallel to the highway) to Artist Point and the upper trailhead leading to the summit of Table Mt. (at the northwest corner of the parking lot). The trail climbs 500' in less than 0.5 mile up the east end of the mountain. Zigzag up through short but exposed lava cliffs—a good place to work on one's fear of heights. The mountain itself is a remnant of an ancient lava flow that was actually deposited in a valley

whose walls have long since eroded away. The path reaches a crest of meadows and panoramic views, and ends at cliffs to the west. Some maps show a trail going down the west end, but it has largely vanished in a rock slide and dangerous snow slope. Best not to descend to Chain Lakes from here.

# 41. Panorama Dome

*Distance: 3 - 4 miles RT*      *Time: Allow 2 - 3 hours*
*Elevation gain: 700 feet*      *Season: July - October*

This short hike through the Mt. Baker Ski Area offers worthwhile views and good berry pickins late summer. From the parking area noted in hike #39 (*map, p. 96*), follow the Wild Goose Trail 0.4 mile to where the trail nears the road. Turn left (may be signed) and cross the road to the well marked trailhead next to a ski lift. The trail drops slightly into Galena Canyon then traverses and climbs Pan Dome to its top. Either turn back here or pass the ski patrol hut to a faint path leading southeast to a small saddle below Shuksan Arm. Curve right (west) and descend to the Lake Ann trailhead at Austin Pass. The Wild Goose Trail is across the paved road for the return.

*Mt. Herman and historic Austin Pass warming hut from Pan Dome.*

# 42. Elbow Lake & Bell Pass

*Distance: 3 - 7 miles RT*          *Time: Allow 2 - 4 hours*
*Elevation gain: 300 - 1,300 feet*   *Season: May - October*

Mid-elevation trailheads offer several pleasant hikes through old-growth forest between Mt. Baker and the Twin Sisters. Elbow Lake is a good fall hike when the bugs aren't so bad. Elbow and tiny Hildebrand and Doreen Lakes nearby are situated at the headwaters of the Middle and South Forks of the Nooksack River. Water flowing north and south from this forested divide allows a major river system to nearly surround the Twin Sisters Range as though it's an island.

There are two approaches to the lakes. The longer north route is accessed from the Middle Fork Road. The southern route is a short easy walk but a much longer drive from Bellingham. Both roads are gated part way from December until mid- to late June to protect elk herds. North approach: turn south off Mt. Baker Highway (MP 16.8) onto the Mosquito Lake Rd., following the latter 4.6 miles to Porter Creek Rd. (USFS Road #38); angle left. In two miles, the North Twin Sister comes

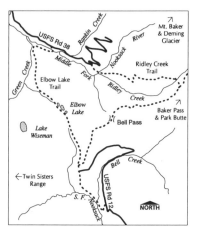

into view (see Middle Fork Nooksack Gorge viewpoint for a possible sidetrip). Stay right at 4.2 miles and left at 4.7 miles (slide area here, road may be rough but is good beyond). At 9 miles is the best view from a road of the mile-wide Sisters Glacier and the South Twin Sister. The seasonal road closure begins near MP 10; the signed trailhead is at 11.4 miles.

Hike down to a footbridge across the river, then continue downstream a long half-mile to where the trail bends south into Green Creek valley. Ascend into a cedar-hemlock forest on a new trail that's replaced most of the old and slippery moss-covered puncheon and stairs. The grade soon lessens and crosses two small streams. At about 2.3 miles from the start, there is a great view of the Green Creek Glacier and the middle peaks of the Sisters Range: (left to right) Cinderella, Little Sister, Skookum and the South Twin Sister (partially hidden). The way heads up Hildebrand Creek, reaching Hildebrand Lake (fast becoming a bog) and Elbow Lake at about 3.5 miles.

South approach: Drive to the end of the South Fork Rd. #12 about 17 miles from Baker Lake Rd. which is reached from Highway 20 near Concrete. (Seasonal road closure is west of Loomis Creek; call the Forest Service for details). The trail to Elbow Lake is an easy 1.5 mile stroll through deep forest along a quiet creek. About 0.2 mile up the trail a right fork leads through stands of large conifers to Bell Pass, about two miles away. In another mile this trail enters subalpine meadows and climbs to Baker Pass and Mt. Baker's spectacular high country 4.3 miles from the start. Note this route is popular with equestrians in late summer and fall.

# 43. Three Lakes & Bear Lake

*Distance: 3.5 - 6 miles RT*      *Time: Allow 3 - 6 hours*
*Elevation gain: 1,200 - 2,000 feet*      *Season: July - October*

It was once possible to drive to the shore of these tiny subalpine lakes by way of mining and logging roads on the southwestern flanks of the Twin Sisters Range. But nature is fast reclaiming the road and returning it to wilderness. This seldom visited corner of the range may offer the best access for exploring its stark beauty and unusual geology. The entire range is composed of olivine-rich dunite, the largest known exposed mass of mantle rock in the Western Hemisphere.

The best approach is an obscure trail from the east by way of Baker Lake (*see hike #42 for directions and a note on road closure*).

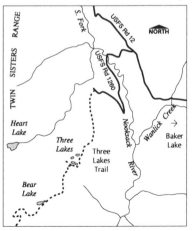

Just past mile 12 on Rd. #12, turn left on Rd. #1260. Cross the South Fork of the Nooksack River and drive or walk to the road end in a clearcut 2 miles beyond (good view of Mt. Baker). The unmarked trail leaves from a high point 150' before the road ends. The path can be hard to follow and a few logs and boulders require some clambering. The lakes (elev. 4,000') are over a

*Rock-flower meadows near Three Lakes.*

ridge crest about 1.7 mile from the trailhead. The trail disappears in meadows so memorize its location. From a collapsed building on the south shore of the larger lake, walk an old road another mile southwest to reach placid Bear Lake.

Some cross-country wandering is possible for experienced navigators. From the first lake, climb 500 feet up boulder and talus slopes (Class 2 rock scrambling), then meadow toward the low point in the ridge due north of the lakes, an excellent overlook of these lakes and Heart Lake in a glacial cirque to the west. This is the southwestern edge of the Mt. Baker Wilderness and the views are exceptional. The area supports a significant elk herd; watch for their large deer-like tracks.

# 44. Shadow of the Sentinels

*Distance: 0.5 Mile RT*     *Time: 1 hour*
*Elevation gain: None*      *Season: Year-round*

"Shadow" is a short walk (0.5 mile) but well worth a visit anytime you're in the Baker Lake area. It is an interpretive nature walk with living exhibits ranging from giant douglas fir trees hundreds of years old to delicate maidenhair ferns sparsely scattered on the forest floor. The self-guided tour includes numerous informative plaques summarizing some of the important ecological relationships that are present in

the forest. Children and adults should enjoy the walk, even on a rainy day. To reach the trailhead, turn left off the North Cascades Highway #20 (after MP 82) onto the Baker Lake Road. The signed parking area is on the right in about 14 miles. The large trail sign includes several historical essays on early inhabitants of the Baker River area, including the legendary prospector-guide, Mr. Joe Morovits. For giant cedar trees, try the Baker River Trail (*hike #52*).

# 45. Baker Hot Springs

*Distance: 0.5 Mile RT*    *Time: 1 hour*
*Elevation gain: None*    *Season: Year-round*

Baker Hot Springs once fed a small cedar-lined pool which had to be destroyed some years ago because of heavy use, abuse and high bacteria counts. However, the 110º springs are unique in the Mt. Baker area and worth a brief dunk anytime. A sizeable pool remains for those whose hike-weary pedestals are in need of a soothing soak.

Turn left off Baker Lake Road (near MP 18) just beyond a bridge onto Road #1130. Follow this 1.6 miles to a junction; stay right. Just before MP 4, turn right on Road #1144. In 0.5 mile there is an informal parking area at the edge of a clear-cut (just past a sharp right bend). Look for the unmarked path up the bank and into the woods. The rough trail quickly improves. It is less than a quarter mile through a deep forest of large cedars, vine maple and devil's club to the sulfurous steaming hot spring. A bit of trivia: it is about 7 miles from here to the steaming Sherman Crater atop Mt. Baker. A rotted "nurse log" nearby supports a precarious row of western hemlock trees. Back at the last road junction, it is only another 0.5 mile to the Rainbow Falls viewpoint, a worthy sidetrip. The old Swift Creek Trailhead is also nearby.

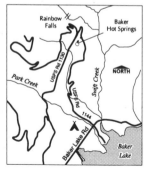

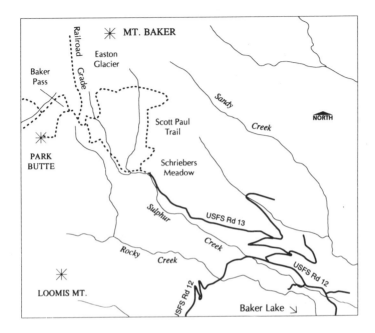

MT. BAKER

Railroad Grade

Easton Glacier

Baker Pass

Scott Paul Trail

PARK BUTTE

NORTH

Sandy Creek

Schriebers Meadow

USFS Rd 13

Sulphur Creek

Rocky Creek

LOOMIS MT.

USFS Rd 12

USFS Rd 12

Baker Lake ↘

*Climber's view of Mt. Baker's summit crater.*

# 46. Scott Paul Trail

*Distance:* 8 miles RT  
*Elevation gain:* 1,800 feet

*Time:* Allow 5 - 7 hours  
*Season:* July - October

For a hike that combines great alpine country with a pleasant saunter through old-growth forest try the new Scott Paul Trail south of Mt. Baker. The trail is a replacement and extension of the old Sulfur Moraine Tail named in the memory of a dear friend to many. Scott, a creative and respected trail planner, designer and builder, left our world prematurely in a trail construction accident, though his gifts to those who love wilderness will be with us for generations.

From North Cascades Hwy (SR 20) turn left at MP 82.2 onto Baker Lake Rd. In 12 miles go left again (Mt. Baker National Recreation Area). In 4.5 miles turn right and reach the trailhead in 5.2 miles (elevation: 3,350'). Hike 50 yards on the trail to Park Butte (*hike #47*) then turn right (signed). The trail gently climbs through an ancient forest of silver fir and occasional hemlock giants. In about 2 miles reach a subalpine ridge with a good view into the Cascades. The trail soon rises above timberline and traverses west through meadow, rock and glacial moraines below the Squak Glacier. After topping out above 5,000 feet, the path begins its descent into the valley of Sulphur Creek, outlet of the massive Easton Glacier just above. Cross a small suspension bridge, and rejoin the Park Butte Trail at a switchback (6 miles to here); stay left (right goes to Morovits Meadows, a huge moraine called the Railroad Grade, and Park Butte). Switchbacks lead down to another bridge and the trailhead a mile beyond.

# 47. Morovits Meadows / Park Butte

*Distance: 5 - 12 miles RT*
*Elevation gain: 1,400 - 2,500 feet*

*Time: Allow 4 - 7 hours*
*Season: July - October*

The trail through Schrieber's Meadow, then up to the upper and lower Morovits Meadows, Baker Pass and Mazama Park offers one of the best hikes in the Mt. Baker area. Expect a lot of company on fair summer weekends (and horses late summer). There are numerous good destinations for a day hike and any number of variations are possible. The views are as dramatic as you'll find anywhere in the Cascades. The lower portion of this trail forms part of an attractive loop with the new Scott Paul Trail (*hike #46*).

*Upper Morovits Meadows, Mazama Park and Mt. Baker.*

See hike #46 for directions to the trailhead at Schrieber's Meadow (*map, p. 106*). An imposing view of the Railroad Grade (a glacial moraine), and the Black Buttes materializes near the trailhead. Head left and cross Sulfur Creek on a bridge, then hike an easy mile of open forest and meadows to several small creek crossings in a broad basin. A removable bridge spans the worst of it (can be treacherous during high runoff without the bridge). The way switchbacks through forest another 1.2 mile to the edge of lower Morovits Meadow just beyond a junction with the Scott Paul Trail.

At a small ridge crest, keep right to view the snout of the Easton Glacier by way of the Railroad Grade, a lateral moraine leading smoothly up to the glacier (climbers' route; watch for marmots). Or follow the main trail 0.5 mile to the upper meadows and Park Butte Trail (left). The lookout atop the 5,400' butte offers an outstanding view of Mt. Baker and the Twin Sisters Range. At the junction, go right for Baker Pass in a mile (the pass can also be reached from the 3.5 mile Ridley Creek Trail at the end of Middle Fork Road). Wander 1.5 mile northwest across Mazama Park to view the immense Deming Gorge (be cautious near the edge, it might not be solid). The

towering Black Buttes, remains of an older volcanic cone, rise in near vertical walls 4,000' above a tumbling mass of ice. Across the gorge look for moving white specks: mountain goats grazing on impossible ledges.

*Marmot watching a marmot watcher*

# 48. Baker Lake

*Distance: 4 - 8 miles RT*
*Elevation gain: 300 feet*

*Time: Allow 2 - 6 hours*
*Season: Almost year-round*

An easy hike along the wild east shore of Baker Lake, this newly rebuilt trail winds through a low-elevation old-growth forest of big trees with good views of Mt. Baker across a ten-mile long reservoir. From Baker Dam (*see hike #49 for directions*), drive about 0.3 mile to a junction and follow Road #1107 another 0.7 mile to the signed trailhead on the left. The trail stays high until crossing Anderson Creek in 1.5 miles. About 0.2 mile beyond a spur drops down to the lake. In summer, it's not unusual to see dark streaks of mud and rock or "lahar" on Mt. Baker's Boulder Glacier emanating from the rim of Sherman Crater. The trail passes old scars from a forest fire suspected of being caused by an 1843 eruption of a now sleeping volcano. At 3.5 miles, another spur descends to the Maple Grove campsite. The East Bank Trail continues six

more miles to Noisy Creek (*see Hike #50*), and three more to Hidden Creek with a final link and new bridge across Baker River scheduled for 1997 (*see map, p. 120*). Total trail length will be about 13 miles with almost year-round access from either end.

*"Koma Kulshan," an icy and active volcano.*

# 49. Watson Lakes & Anderson Butte

*Distance: 3 - 8 miles RT*          *Time: Allow 2 - 6 hours*
*Elevation gain: 1,000 - 2,000 feet*     *Season: July - October*

Once you arrive at these two peaceful lakes, you may have a way hard time leaving. They are sizeable gems surrounded by fairy tale parklands as each bend in the trail reveals another placid scene. Autumn is very nice: brilliant red huckleberry leaves against still water reflecting tall trees and sky.

From Highway 20 (MP 82.2), head north on the Baker Lake Rd. about 13 miles, then turn right on Rd. 1106, crossing Baker Dam in another 1.5 miles. Turn left on Rd. #1107 (sign) and continue 9 more miles to a spur (sign); turn left to reach the new trailhead in a short mile (elevation 4,500'). The trail climbs 400 feet through hemlock-silver fir forest and in less than a mile passes the Anderson Butte Trail (left) at the start of a long rising meadow (Mt. Baker looms off your right shoulder half way up). The old lookout site and fine viewing perch on top of the butte are another 0.7 mile and 500 feet higher. From the rising meadow the main trail descends 100 feet in forest and intersects the Anderson Lakes Trail (right) at 1.5 miles. This optional side trip traverses a green rock garden and in 0.5 mile reaches a sizeable lake, sprawling meadows, and abundant late-summer huckleberries. Another fab view of Mt. Baker is from across the lake's outlet stream.

From the junction, the trail to Watson Lakes gains another 100 feet to a saddle at the edge of the Noisy-Diobsud Wilderness, then quickly descends 400 feet to a campsite at the first lake.

*Watson Lakes.*

Work left along the shore, clambering over a few logs, heading toward a beautiful isthmus of subalpine knolls between the two lakes (privy nearby). The second lake is much larger and has a dramatic shoreline, including enchanted meadows and the high cliffs of Mt. Watson. Snowy Bacon Peak rises to the east; Anderson Butte is to the north (imagine the view). It's about 2.5 miles from the trailhead to the lower lake, and despite the ups and downs, a suitable hike for families. Not surprisingly, the trail is kinda popular on summer weekends.

# 50. Noisy Creek

*Distance: 2 to 10 miles RT*          *Time: Allow 2 - 6 hours*
*Elevation gain: 100 - 1,200 feet*      *Season: April - November*

Noisy Creek was the focus of years of controversy over the potential logging of an exceptional ancient forest along the creek's lower reach which was recognized as an important ecosystem by the public, and a valuable timber resource by the landowners. In 1990, the Nature Conservancy, Congress and the U.S. Forest Service came to the rescue. Surrounded by National Forest and Wilderness, the big trees are now secure from the historic assault on Pacific Northwest old-growth forests.

The trailhead can be reached by small boat, or by walking the Baker Lake Trail from either end (*see Hike #43 for directions*). It's about 4.5 miles to Noisy Creek from the north, or about 9.5 miles from the southerly trailhead. For the easiest access, you can cross the lake by boat from Shannon Creek Campground. Noisy Creek flows down the largest valley directly across the lake, about 0.8 mile away and marked by a wide area of gravel, cobbles and boulders (an alluvial fan). Disembark and head left on the Baker Lake Trail nearby to find the inconspicuous Noisy Creek Trail on the right at the crest of a ridge shoulder just east of the creek. The route leads away from the stream and is moderately steep, gaining 700 feet in the first mile. Along the lower stretch you will find a huge douglas fir tree, over ten feet in diameter. Western hemlock and red cedar stand where they've been standing since before the first whites arrived on the continent. The noisy cascading stream is reached again at about 1.5 mile; enjoy the view—and the "noise." This is a good viewpoint and turn-around. Osprey, eagles and spotted owls are known to inhabit the area.

# The North Cascades

# 51. Nooksack Cirque

*Distance: 7 - 13 miles RT*          *Time: Allow 4 - 9 hours*
*Elevation gain: 500 - 1000 feet*          *Season: August - October*

This adventurous route requires a ford at the beginning across Ruth Creek and should not be attempted at high water. One of these years the Forest Service plans to replace the bridge over the creek and link it to a proposed nature trail along the Ruth Gorge. The hike is unique and best done late in the summer or fall when runoff is low and you can walk river bars much of the way. Despite inconvenient access and irregular maintenance, the route is still worth exploring.

The North Fork of the Nooksack River finds its roots in the meltwater of Mt. Shuksan's northern glaciers. Towering walls of rock and ice form a mile-wide glacial cirque at the head of the river where ambitious hikers are rewarded with outstanding views for their efforts. Although the elevation gain is not great, the approach can be tedious.

From Mt. Baker Highway (MP 46.5) turn left on Hannegan Rd. (#32) just before a bridge (*map, p. 88*). Stay right at a fork in 1.3 mile and continue about 1 mile to the trailhead where the bridge used to be (elevation 2300'). If it's safe, cross, remembering that streams fed by snow and icemelt, usually rise during the day and fall overnight. Enjoy the view of Shuksan, and walk the smooth gravel road 1.6 mile to the old trailhead which leads down an overgrown logging road. In another .8 mile, the path enters a forest of large old trees, some of which are strewn across the trail sprouting mushrooms and impeding your progress. The river and gravel bars are reached 3.5 miles from the start. From here, a worse trail continues intermittently, close to the bank through brush and over logs and side channels. However, the recommended route is up the river bed itself. This can only be done, of course, during low run-off when the river is down. September and October are the best months for low water and fall colors. (Early spring during a cool dry spell may also be good.)

When the gravel bars are negotiable, simply wander as far up the valley as you like, carefully marking and remembering the place you entered the river bed so you don't miss it on the return hike. It is another 2.5 to 3 miles to the best views deep in the cirque, although the scene is scenic all along the way. Icy Peak, Jagged Ridge and the East Nooksack Glacier dominate the skyline. Just beyond the point where a forested area ends on the left, it may be easiest to follow a series of dry side channels that parallel the river on the left side. The final mile is more difficult due to the narrowing stream bed and a stubborn patch of brush. When open gentle slopes scattered

with boulders become visible (also on the left), head toward a house-sized overhanging boulder. The view is excellent. Seahpo Peak and the sheer Nooksack Tower pierce the sky. On the river, a certain amount of boulder-hopping can be expected. A walking stick offers defense against wet rocks and slippery logs. An extra pair of wool socks might also come in handy.

*Old-growth forest.*

# 52. Baker River

*Distance: 2 - 5 miles RT*        *Time: Allow 23 - 4 hours*
*Elevation gain: 50 - 200 feet*        *Season: Almost year-round*

When winters are mild, this easy trail may be open year-round since it never exceeds 1,000' in elevation. Early mornings are the best time to enjoy the river, large beaver ponds and the veritable rainforest of giant western red cedar and big leaf maple. A low angle sun on a clear morning reflects brilliantly through the rich green moss and shaded ferns on the forest floor. The walk is relaxed and suitable for almost anyone, (unless blocked by the occasional slide or washout which might require a minor detour). The first mile can generally be

*More old-growth: Baker River's temperate rainforest.*

negotiated by wheelchairs. The trail enters North Cascades National Park so pets are not allowed.

Turn left off the North Cascades Highway #20 (MP 82.4) onto the Baker Lake Road. Drive 26 miles (mostly paved), making a left near the road end (*map, p. 120*). The trailhead is well marked. From the river bank, Mt. Hagan is visible high above. Several footlogs are crossed as you enter a seemingly enchanted forest of giant cedars (up to 12' diameter). Sword ferns (the largest), deer and lady ferns dominate the ground cover, but other ferns and numerous shade-tolerant flowering plants like trillium, wild ginger and bleeding hearts thrive in the damp environment. From 1.5 to 2 miles in, extensive beaver ponds are passed, offering a good opportunity to observe wildlife if you're quiet, patient and inconspicuous. A camp at Sulphide Creek is reached in 2.5 miles.

In early summer, the creek is torrential from snowmelt originating in the high cirque of Mt. Shuksan's Sulphide and Crystal Glaciers to the northwest. Cloudcap (or Seahpo) Peak and Jagged Ridge are visible to the north. Later in summer or autumn, when the level of the creek has fallen, it may be possible to walk out onto gravel bars for much better views and a sunny lunch spot. A faint path leading upstream along the edge of the woods may offer access to the broad creek bed. If Sulphide Creek can be crossed safely, remnants of an old trail heading farther up the Baker River valley could be scouted by more experienced trekkers.

# 53. Shuksan Lake

*Distance: 4 - 6 miles RT*　　　　*Time: Allow 3 - 7 hours*
*Elevation gain: 1,500 - 2,500 feet*　*Season: July - October*

A shorter, scenic but strenuous hike, the trail to Shuksan and Little Shuksan Lakes is steeper than any other listed in this guide. Nevertheless, three lovely lakes and unique views into some of the wilder parts of the North Cascades are worth the beating getting there. Overnight prospects are also good.

To find the trail, drive Baker Lake Rd north from Highway 20 about 24 miles to Rd #1160; turn left. Follow this winding

*October snow.*

gravel road to its end 4 miles up where views of Mt. Baker and Baker Lake offer encouragement for the work yet to be done. The trail is tucked in the bushes and bypasses a few false starts in the first 100 yards then becomes more obvious as you leave the old clearcut. With only a couple of rests the trail stays steep to the top of the ridge, passing a nice view of Mts. Hagan and Blum. At a short rock scramble, go up and a little left to find the trail. From the meadowy crest, Little Shuksan Lake is visible 300 feet below. Hike down to the lake and continue around its west side to another tiny lake (trail is faint so memorize the way). At a junction in meadows just beyond, angle right for the grand view: Mt. Shuksan's seldom seen Sulphide and Crystal Glaciers, Jagged Ridge, Cloudcap Peak, the Baker River valley, Blum, Hagan, and Bacon Peak.

From the junction go left on a fainter path to explore meadows, or go straight ahead for the 600-foot descent through very steep terrrain to the larger Shuksan Lake nestled in a remote canyon below. The trail is rough and may be hard to follow, to the delight of every devout fisherperson. Bears are common in the area, as are several varierites of huckleberries later in summer.

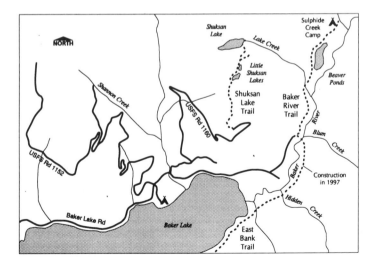

# 54. Thornton Lakes & Trapper Peak

*Distance: 10 - 12 miles RT*      *Time: Allow 6 - 9 hours*
*Elevation gain: 2,600 - 3,600 feet*    *Season: July - September*

Despite a moderately steep approach to the lakes, the views from the top of Trapper Ridge are worth the effort. The lakes require a steep 450 foot descent after a long hike up the mountain, although the cool water is a treat on a hot day.

About 12 miles northeast of Marblemount, turn left (north) off the North Cascades Highway #20 (MP 117.3) onto the signed gravel road paralleling the highway. In 5 miles, the road is blocked where the hike begins (elevation 2700'). Follow the

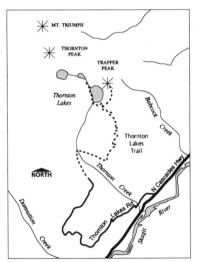

old road bed through a large clearcut and across Thornton Creek in a mile. At 2 miles watch carefully for the marked trail on the left side of the old road. Follow this through dense forest gaining 2,000 feet in the next 2.5 miles. Just before the crest of the ridge (and a view of the first lake) a faint path to the right follows this scenic ridge northward 0.7 mile to the summit of Trappers Peak 1,000 feet higher.

*Water moves.*

Views of the Skagit River, Mt. Triumph and the jagged Picket Range are humbling. One September afternoon the author, a friend, and four bears surprised each other at close range while the six of us were feeding on huckleberries. From the trailhead to summit, it's about 5.3 miles with a gain of 3200 feet. Back where the main trail overlooks the lake, scramble down a steep, blasted (literally) trail 450 feet to this largest of the three lakes. Another faint path leads through a campsite and along the west shore to the outlet of the middle lake. Ambitious hikers can explore the upper lakes or the high rocky ridge on their south rim. Or, for a view of the Triumph Glacier, climb the climbers' path to a saddle northwest of the middle lake (dangerous beyond this point).

# 55. Stetattle Creek

*Distance: 4 - 7 miles RT*          *Time: Allow 2 - 4 hours*
*Elevation gain: 500 - 800 feet*     *Season: April - November*

A pretty waterfall and views of Pyramid and Colonial peaks are the main attractions of this trip. This trail doesn't receive a lot of use, but is in good condition and is an enjoyable wilderness walk early or late in the summer season. The well marked trailhead is at Diablo, elevation 900 feet (*map, next page*). Turn left off Highway #20 before the Gorge Lake bridge (MP 126) and in 0.7 mile park just beyond the Stetattle Creek bridge. The path hugs the edge of the creek behind a residential area before entering the woods. A few short switchbacks are encountered in the first mile and several small streams are crossed. Bucket Creek Falls is reached in about 2 miles (elevation 1400 feet). Looking back down the valley from the opposite side of the creek, there are good views of Pyramid and Colonial Peaks across the Skagit gorge.

One can turn around here or continue several miles up valley. More streams are crossed (may not be possible during high runoff) and the tread becomes fainter at each crossing. In about 1.5 miles beyond the falls, the huge rock walls of the northeast face of Davis Peak come into view through the trees. The old trail becomes obscured by brush and fallen trees so rather than losing it, a turn-around may be in order. The valley is essentially untouched wilderness and was once a common route for mountaineers on their way into the Picket Range. (For a 5,200 foot grunt to gorgeous views and an old fire lookout, try the Sourdough Mt. Trail nearby to the east.)

# 56. Pyramid Lake

*Distance: 4 miles RT*        *Time: 2.5 - 3 hours*
*Elevation gain: 1,500 feet*        *Season: May - October*

This attractive lake is at 2600 feet elevation so the trail is free
of snow much earlier in the year than many other areas of the
Park. Although the scenery is not spectacular, the lake is nice
and the trail is worthwhile for restless hikers looking for an
early season conditioner. The signed trailhead is located on
the south side of Highway 20 at Pyramid Creek (MP 126.8).

The path immediately gains a ridge crest and passes through
a large stand of lodgepole pine. In less than a mile, the creek
draining the lake is crossed in an area of big cedars. The trail
follows the creek valley in a forest of more typical cedar and
douglas fir. Plenty of berries line the path later in summer.
The trail passes a huge leaning fir just before the final short
steep climb to the lake, a mile beyond the creek crossing. A

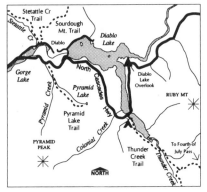

comfortable resting
place is hard to find
unless a good log is
available that doesn't
float away when you
step on it. An improved
view of the lake and
Pyramid Peak can be
found by scrambling up
to the left (northeast) a
few yards over loose
rock.

# 57. Thunder Creek & 4th of July Pass

*Distance: 1.5 - 10 miles RT*            *Time: Allow 1 - 5 hours*
*Elevation gain: 500 - 2,400 feet*       *Season: May - October*

Near Diablo Lake, the trail up this broad valley is an easy walk and leads to a number of popular destinations in the National Park. A nature trail and historic river crossing offer short, easy walks, while Fourth of July Pass is a moderate climb up the southwest side of Ruby Mountain.

Drive to the Colonial Creek Campground on the south side of Highway 20 at Diablo Lake (MP 130.1). The trail begins on a grassy slope just above the big parking lot. Just before a bridge crosses Thunder Creek in 1.2 mile, an optional mile long nature walk loops up and right through the forest. An historical sign describes the former bridge whose rotted piling can still be seen nearby. The trail to Fourth of July Pass is on the left 0.7 mile after the bridge. The Pass is a moderate 2,300-foot climb over 3 miles. After the first mile the going gets easier, steepening again in the last mile. At Fourth of July camp Colonial and Snowfield Peaks are visible across the valley. Continuing on, Panther Potholes (ponds) are seen below on the right and a wet forested saddle is reached. The Panther Creek Trail descends 5.5 miles to Highway 20 at the east end of Ruby Arm, 9 miles from Colonial Campground.

On the Thunder Creek Trail, one can hike upstream 3 or 4 miles to better mountain views. Overnight trips to Park Creek Pass are possible as are numerous other alternatives. Consult other guidebooks and the Park Service for details.

# 58. Little Jack Mountain

*Distance: 12 - 16 miles RT*      *Time: Allow 7 - 10 hours*
*Elevation gain: 4,000 - 5,400 feet*      *Season: June - October*

All the high ground along this trail is south-facing which
allows the winter snowpack to recede quickly, sometimes by
late May (no guarantees). That in turn makes this one of the
best early summer hikes to the North Cascades' totally
awesome alpine country. Wildflowers may be early too. The
views are exceptional anytime. Water's scarce so carry plenty.

The Little Jack Trail begins at a junction with the East Bank
Trail at Ross Lake. Find the trailhead just east of the lake on
the north side of Highway 20 about 4.5 miles beyond the Ross
Dam Trailhead (*see p. 160*). Hike the East Bank Trail down to

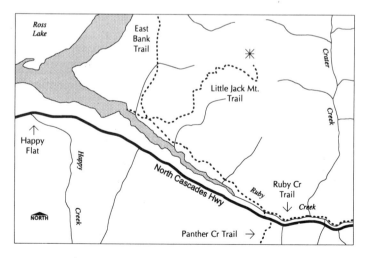

*Ross Lake from Little Jack Mt. Trail.*

a bridge across Ruby Creek (Ruby Creek Trail goes right, a pleasant 3 mile stroll to the trailhead for Crater Mt.; *see Hike #57*). Stay left and follow mostly easy grade about 2.6 miles to the Little Jack junction. Turn right and follow this trail up and east turning dozens of switchbacks on the climb to timberline. Views of neighboring peaks and Ross Lake glimmering below steadily improve on the ascent to a camp near the ridge crest about 5 miles from the junction. If there's energy left, wander up the ridge another mile (700 feet of vertical) for all the good views, including Jack and Crater Mountains to the north and east. Turn back when faded trail, rough terrain, or deep snow make the going too tough.

# 59. Crater Lake & Lookout

*Distance: 11 - 15 miles RT*    *Time: Allow 7 - 10 hours*
*Elevation gain: 4,000 - 5,400 feet*    *Season: July - October*

This is a strenuous day trip also suited to a two or three day overnighter for experienced backpackers. The high cirque of Crater Mt. guarding this tiny lake plus excellent views of near and distant peaks offer sufficient rewards for the effort it takes to get there. Water can be scarce in late season.

The trailhead is east of Ross Lake at the confluence of Granite and Canyon Creek, just east of MP 141 on the North Cascades Highway #20. From the parking lot (elev: 1900'), follow the Canyon Creek Trail 0.2 mile to cross the footbridge over Granite Creek and stay left to reach a new bridge over Canyon Creek in another 0.2 mile. Once across Canyon Creek, follow the Devils Park/Crater Mt. Trail east (upstream) and north through what seems like endless forest switchbacks with

occasional views and a few small stream crossings along the way. At 4.2 miles and 3,400 feet from the start a junction in subalpine meadows of McMillan Park is reached. Stay left for Crater Lake (at 5,800 feet) in less than a mile. A huge wall of rock surrounds the lake which is generally snow-free by mid-July. For great views, head leftward near the lake and 300 feet up to the crest of a low ridge to the southwest (several

*Ruby Creek near Crater Mt. trailhead.*

campsites). With a few energy bars one can hike an old fire
lookout trail, if it's snow-free, along this ridge another 2 miles
and 1500' gain nearly to the summit of Crater Mt. and
maximum views. The trail ends at a series of dangerous cliffs
(class 3 rock climbing for mountaineers). At the lake, the right
path leads 2 miles to another old lookout site (elevation 7,054')
offering good views of Jerry Glacier, Jerry Lakes and Jack Mt.
At the McMillan Park junction, the Devils Park Trail is good
for multi-day trips, including a 43-mile loop around Jack Mt.
(Consult the other hiking guides listed in the introduction.)

# 60. Hart's Pass to Grasshopper Pass

*Distance:  8 - 12 miles RT*  *Time:  Allow 5 - 8 hours*
*Elevation gain:  500 - 1,000 feet*  *Season:  July - October*

This is an outstanding day hike on one of the finest segments
of the Pacific Crest Trail in the North Cascades.  The trailhead
is very high (6,500 feet) and elevation gain is minimal.  The
Crest Trail extends from Mexico to Canada and the route
through the North Cascades of Washington State is superb.
Longer trips are often made between Rainy Pass on Highway
20 to Manning Park in British Columbia.  Several guidebooks
can be consulted to learn the details of such a trip.

For a day hike, drive Highway 20 over Washington Pass to
Mazama, turning north at MP 186 (60 miles east of
Newhalem).  In 0.5 mile turn left and follow the signs 19 miles
to Hart's Pass (elevation 6,200′).  The gravel road is steep,
narrow and winding, but usually in good condition.  At the

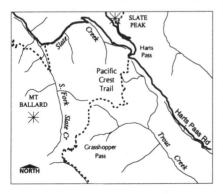

pass, turn left to reach
a campground and the
trailhead just beyond
at the road end.  Hike
through trees then
contour the open
slopes up to a small
saddle at the ridge crest
for the first good views.
Robinson Mountain
dominates the scene to
the northeast.

130

*PCT near Grasshopper Pass.*

The trail gently gains another 400 feet, climbing around a minor summit to another crest at 7,000 feet, about 2.3 miles from the start. Continuing west, Tatie Peak is passed on the south and a saddle is reached just beyond. An easy rock scramble leads up from here to Tatie's 7,386-foot summit. On a clear day, the top of Mt. Baker is visible far in the west.

The trail turns south, drops over a ridge, descends then climbs a bit to open meadows at Grasshopper Pass. Azurite Peak and Mt. Ballard tower high to the southwest and northwest across the South Fork of Slate Creek. The steep trail to Glacier Pass is visible below (not recommended for a day hike). The ridge crest to the south makes a nice saunter. This ridge system is the divide between the Skagit and Columbia River watersheds, it is the crest of the Cascade Range, and the line between Whatcom and Okanogan Counties. Due to high elevation, the road and trail are often snow covered into July.

# 61. Chilliwack River

*Distance: 5 - 14 miles RT*  *Time: Allow 3 - 8 hours*
*Elevation gain: 100 - 500 feet*  *Season: April - November*

Few folks from outside Canada ever visit Chilliwack Lake, a spectacular gem, eh, in a wild and rugged setting. The rough trail up the river that feeds the lake penetrates a classic ancient forest of giant cedar and fir, and leads to North Cascades National Park, less than 2 miles in (backcountry permit may be required for the border crossing). Call the NCNP office in Sedro Woolley for information (360-856-5700).

From Bellingham, drive Mt. Baker Highway and Highway 9 to the border crossing at Sumas. Continue north to the Trans-Canada Highway (#1) then east to Chilliwack. Take the

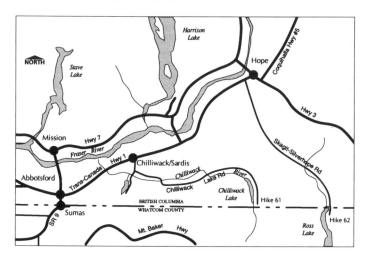

*Chilliwack River from Little Chilliwack Camp.*

Chilliwack-Sardis exit and go south to the Chilliwack River bridge; turn left before crossing. Follow this road to its end at the south end of Chilliwack Lake, two hours from Bellingham (stay right at Paleface and Depot Creeks). Walk the old road 200 yards to the trail on your left. The path enters a grove of mature cedar, then hardwoods, then bigger cedars (up to 10 feet across). Walk as far as you like, negotiating fallen logs, occasional brush, and footlogs over small streams (some may be difficult). Reach the border at 1.7 miles. Beyond, the trail passes several camps and gradually improves as it climbs to junctions with Copper Lake, Hannegan Pass and Whatcom Pass trails (all overnight trips). An exciting suspension bridge crosses Indian Creek seven miles up. Brush is worst mid-June to mid-September. And watch out for bears, eh.

# 62. Hozomeen Lake & Willow Lake

*Distance: 7.5 - 11.5 miles RT*  *Time: Allow 4 - 8 hours*
*Elevation gain: 300 - 1000 feet*  *Season: May - November*

The remote north end of Ross Lake is seldom visited by Whatcom Countians. This is the northern segment of a trail that runs the entire length of Ross Lake, ending at Ruby Creek and Highway 20. From Bellingham, access to this scenic blitz (save it for a sunny day) is by way of Hope, B.C., an hour and a half drive from Bellingham. Just before Hope and the bridge across Silverhope Creek, turn right on the Skagit-Silverhope Road to Ross Lake (*map, p. 132*). Drive another 39 miles, crossing the border into North Cascades National Park. There is a short interpretive trail worth visiting at the international boundary near the park entrance station.

Find the well marked lakes trailhead in the campground area (usually full on summer weekends). This is the primary hike to be done from this end of Ross Lake so the trail is well maintained to both lakes. The trail climbs through forest south of Hozomeen Creek, gaining nearly a thousand feet in three miles, where a junction is reached. Hozomeen Lake is an easy half-mile up the spur trail (left). The views of the towering summits of Hozomeen Peak from the lake shore are no less than spectacular. All three peaks had been climbed by 1951. From the junction it is another 2 miles and a measly 200 foot gain to Willow Lake, tucked in a canyon due north of Desolation Peak. Beyond, the trail drops into the long crescent valley of Lightning Creek between Skagit and Desolation Peaks (the latter a famous Jack Kerouac retreat).

# Other Trails

*We are fortunate in Whatcom County to have a great selection of trails in the Cascades and in the city of Bellingham. What's missing are more public trail opportunities in the lowlands and the foothills. While many unofficial trails do exist in these areas, they often cross private land which tends to limit their accessibility to the public. The potential trails noted in the Foreword would go a long way toward resolving this problem if we could secure funding and work out arrangements with landowners to get these trails built.*

The following trails are generally open to the public although some may be subject to landowner permission:

## Sumas Mountain/Lost Lake

Outstanding views of the Nooksack and Fraser River valleys at the end of a 2,400-foot climb up the northwest side of the mountain. Two trails off South Pass Road are good, but both currently cross private land at the start and use may be restricted. State or County acquisition or easement, some trail realignment, and parking and trailhead improvements are needed for the public to fully enjoy this exceptional area.

## Lummi Mountain

Two routes 1,500 feet up the north and east sides of Lummi Mountain both cross private lands and public access may be limited. Views west into the San Juan Islands are fantastic. The entire south end of Lummi Island is unique in Whatcom County and has the potential for an excellent wilderness trail system utilizing old road beds and some new trails. Sensitive wildlife habitat requires special care in locating any new trail.

## Portage Island

Off the end of Lummi Peninsula, this undeveloped island is physically accessible to hikers at low tide and a loop around the island on an old road grade offers good potential. The story goes that the Lummi Tribe is supposed to develop the island as a public park and natural area as part of a settlement reached with Whatcom County some years ago. The County owned the island but had no legal access and was forced to give it up. Cultural resources do need to be protected, but so far the county hasn't seriously challenged the tribe or the federal government regarding access.

## Lummi River Dikes

This area is also within the Lummi Indian Reservation and access may be limited. From the Red River Road, miles of dikes stretch across the delta of the historic mouth of the Nooksack River. Bird life is a strong attraction and winter walks are enjoyable.

## Samish Bay Dikes (Skagit County)

The large delta adjoining Samish and Padilla Bays in Skagit County attracts thousands of waterfowl in winter, most notably large flocks of brant geese. The dikes that protect farmland from inundating high tides offer good access to the delta for viewing birds and sunsets. A brushy approach to an otherwise walkable dike is off the south end of the Colony Creek bridge on Chuckanut Drive (SR 11) at the northern edge of the delta. The brush may be bypassed on rocks and marine vegetation if the tide isn't too high. The dike wanders around many small points and coves for three miles to Edison (see Harvey Manning's *Walking the Beach to Bellingham* for more info.). If hunters are a-hunting, don't scare off the ducks, although the latter might appreciate the unarmed company.

## Chuckanut Mountain/South Bellingham

A future trail network may connect existing trails and park facilities into a hiker's haven of urban wilderness. Numerous route connections are feasible: Larrabee, Arroyo and Fairhaven Parks, the Interurban Trail, the north Lost Lake and Chuckanut Ridge trails, Fragrance Lake, Cody Ridge, Pine and Cedar Lakes, and other sites, many of which are under increasing stress from new and proposed development. Many old logging roads and user trails can be found throughout the Chuckanuts that aren't described here, but which offer great opportunities (*see map next page*). Hiker-only designations are expected for troubled trails where user conflicts and damage to soils and vegetation can't be resolved.

## Lookout/Galbraith Mountain

As with Chuckanut Mountain, this area is criss-crossed with many old logging grades and user trails within a large urban wilderness setting. Connections from Whatcom Falls Park to Lake Padden, Lake Whatcom, and even Lake Samish are possibilities. A north-south corridor was identified by the Bellingham Greenways program established to acquire critical open space and trail easements in the city.

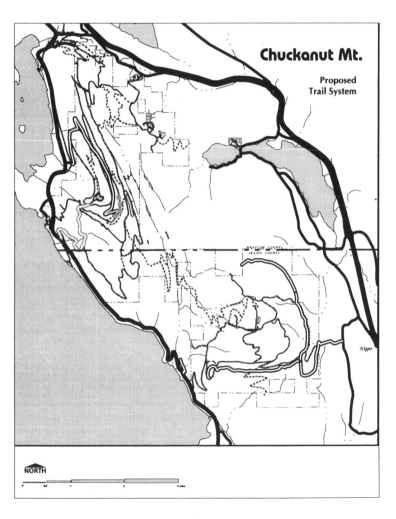

# Chuckanut Mt.

**Proposed Trail System**

WHATCOM COUNTY
SKAGIT COUNTY

Alger

NORTH

## Stewart Mountain

This 3,000-foot high ridge above the northeast shore of Lake Whatcom supports a few trails, old logging roads and a powerline corridor presenting obvious possibilities to the hiker. The powerline is not the prettiest and much of the area is private, but views of the lake and the North Cascades make exploration worthwhile. Access is off the end of North Shore Road, Y Road, or the DNR logging road off Highway 9 north of Wickersham. Potential routes connect nicely with the Lake Whatcom Trail and the undeveloped county park site at Smith Creek and North Shore Road.

## Mt. Baker and the North Cascades

The number of hikes in the North Cascades far exceeds the space limitations of this book. There are many excellent trails in the Mt. Baker area which may or may not be described in other books. A few are: Skyline Divide, Bastille Ridge, Canyon Ridge, Keep Kool Trail, Gold Run Pass/Tomyhoi Lake, Copper Ridge, Lake Ann, Shuksan Arm, Swift Creek, Lava Divide, Boulder Ridge, Blue Lake, Dock Butte, Wanlick Creek, Upper South Fork Nooksack, Bell Pass and Ridley Creek. In the North Cascades beyond Mt. Baker you will find Whatcom Pass, Easy Ridge, Little and Big Beaver Valleys, East Bank Ross Lake, Devil's Dome, Sourdough Ridge, Canyon Creek, Three Fools, and the Pacific Crest Trail. The Forest Service and National Park Service can be consulted for information on these areas (see listings in the back of the book).

# Parks

*Peace Arch.*

## 1. Lighthouse Marine Park (Pt. Roberts)

This 22-acre park on the tip of a four square-mile peninsula overlooks the Strait of Georgia and the Gulf Islands of British Columbia. You'll find boardwalks, creative covered picnic facilities, a view tower, boat ramps and campsites adjacent to a half-mile of sandy marine beach. Short beach walks are possible any time. Occasionally in spring grey whales may be seen migrating offshore, while orcas are more common. In August plan to attend the annual arts and crafts festival at the park which has become a major summer event drawing thousands of people from B.C. and Washington State.

*Directions:* The only road access to Pt. Roberts is through Canada. From the Blaine I-5 border crossing, follow BC Highway #1 (99) about 13 miles north to the Tsawwassen exit. Head west across the freeway overpass, stay on Highway #17, and follow the signs to the Point. When you cross the border again, continue straight ahead then curve right around a marina, reaching the park in another half-mile.

## 2. Peace Arch State Park (Blaine)

At the Blaine I-5 border crossing, Canadian and Washington State park agencies maintain extensive lawns and gardens converging on the Peace Arch. The Arch was built in 1914 with money raised by kids to commemorate the lasting friendship between the two countries. Take exit 274 and follow signs a short way to the northeast. Also visit Blaine Harbor west of I-5 and look for the new trail and viewing areas along the waterfront.

## 3.  Semiahmoo Park (Blaine)

The county's newest park, Semiahmoo is located on the narrow neck of a unique 1.3 mile long sandy spit. This unusual landform was naturally constructed by currents that bring sediments northward from high eroding bluffs to the south. At its narrowest point, opposing beaches are only yards apart, certainly an odd place for a road. At the turn of the century, a large fish cannery and company sailing port occupied the spit (some structures still exist). The interpretive facilities and historical library at the park illustrate those memories well. Canoe rentals are sometimes available for exploring the protected waters of Drayton Harbor and the Blaine Marina, and clam shovels may be available. Directions: Take I-5 exit 272 to Portal Way, then immediately turn left on Blaine Rd. Follow the signs to Semiahmoo Resort. (See also walk #2, Semiahmoo Spit.)

## 4.  Birch Bay State Park

Fortunately, this park was established before the beach could be developed with a crowd of vacation cottages like those that line much of the bay to the north. A mile of sunny beaches and warmish water makes this a gem among marine parks. In summer, thousands of visitors fill the entire community, so early morning, weekday or off-season visits are recommended. Campsites, restrooms, and countless picnic tables and grills are available. The variety of bird life is amazing in winter and spring. See walk #4, Birch Bay to Cherry Point, for directions.

*Berthusen Park.*

## 5. Berthusen Park (Lynden)

Managed by the City of Lynden, this small forest preserve was donated to the city by Hans and Lida Berthusen in their will. Several paths through a grove of old-growth douglas fir and cedar offers a rare glimpse of the great temperate rainforest conifers that once covered much of the Whatcom Basin. The understory is missing, so you can enjoy these trees up close. Old farm equipment is also on display. Head north of Lynden on the Guide Meridian, then left on the Badger Road a mile, turning left again on Berthusen Road and right into the park.

## 6.   Tennant Lake/Hovander Homestead Parks (Ferndale)

See walk #25 for information and directions to this important nature preserve and historical site. Interpretive facilities, a fragrant herb garden with labels in braille, view towers, boardwalk trail through a swampy lakeshore, a nicely preserved turn-of-the-century barn and farmhouse, and summer cultural events like the Scottish Highland Games and international folkdancing highlight these adjoining Whatcom County parks just south of Ferndale.

## 7.   Cornwall Park (Bellingham)

This 65-acre park set in maturing forest has a fitness trail, picnic areas, lawns, tennis courts, a rose garden and the babbling waters of Squalicum Creek flowing through its north end. The park is located east of Meridian and north of Illinois St. Eventually, the Bay-To-Baker Trail may connect the park with Bug Lake and Sunset Pond to the east and the proposed Little Squalicum Park to the west.

## 8.   Maritime Heritage Park (Bellingham)

This park, marine center and salmon hatchery has become the largest public greenspace and recreation site in the downtown area. Paved trails, viewpoints and a pedestrian bridge below lower Whatcom Falls provide great access to Whatcom Creek (watch for spawning salmon in the fall). Boardwalks and other improvements have been proposed by the city to connect with Citizens Dock and Squalicum Harbor. The park is located between Prospect and West Holly (*see walk #9*).

## 9. Harbor Point Park (Bellingham)

A recent addition to the Bellingham park system is Harbor Point Park, a Port of Bellingham facility at Squalicum Harbor. Attractions include nicely maintained lawns, benches overlooking Bellingham Bay, a memorial to lost fishermen, and a paved walkway connecting with extensive bicycle and pedestrian facilities around the harbor. Find the park on a point of land west of the marina and south of Harbor Mall.

## 10. Whatcom Falls Park (Bellingham)

See hike #10 for information about this 241 acre "urban wilderness" city park. Several beautiful waterfalls, maturing forest, hiking and biking trails, bridges, play and picnic areas, a kids' fishing pond, and a state fish hatchery make this an attractive destination. Located near the intersection of Lakeway Dr. and Electric Ave. Watch for the new trail system to be constructed along Whatcom Creek from the park to downtown over the next several years.

## 11. Lake Padden Park (Bellingham)

The city's largest park (over 1,000 acres) includes a championship 18-hole golf course, a lake nearly a mile long, ten miles of horse, bike and hiking trails, ballfields, picnic areas, shelters, showers, boat launch (non-motorized) and other recreation facilities. See walk #16 and hike #17 for several enjoyable walks around the lake. The park is located on the south side of Samish Way about two miles southeast of its intersection with I-5 in Bellingham.

## 12. Samish Park

The first Whatcom County Park has a quarter mile of lake front and is great for swimming, canoe paddling and picnicking. Canoes and pedal boats are often rentable in summer. A quiet trail wanders the lakeshore to the west and another climbs north to an overlook. From I-5 exit 246, follow North Lake Samish Rd. to the park on the right.

## 13. Larrabee State Park

Washington's first state park, Larrabee is one of the finest marine parks in the Northwest. The dramatic rocky shoreline borders a verdant forest of old and tall douglas fir, western red cedar, madrone and big cottonwoods. Picnic shelters and tables, boat launch, many campsites, two mountain lakes, scenic viewpoints, and at least twenty miles of hiking trails (and the potential for a lot more) make this a great place to visit many times over. Several paths give access to tide pools at low water. See walk #7, hikes #18, 19 and 20, and viewpoint #12 for additional information. The park is 5 miles south of Fairhaven on Chuckanut Drive (SR 11).

## 14. Silver Lake Park (Maple Falls)

This scenic 400 acre park is considered by some to be the finest county park. The steep forested slopes of Black Mountain rise above the opposite shore, while the slightly rolling forest and lawns within the park offer good camping, picnicking, creative lounging, and aimless wandering on lonely forest paths and a boardwalk and bridge across a shallow bay. Several rustic and inviting cabins are perched above the shoreline, but you'll likely need a reservation, except maybe on a weekday in the off season. The historic, beautifully crafted Gerdrum House stands against Red Mountain to the west. The park makes a great base camp for other hiking areas in the region north of Mt. Baker. Group picnic areas, children's play areas, a boat launch (under 10hp), horse stables and camps, fishing, swimming, showers, and paddling are also available. Drive 31 miles east of Bellingham on the Mt. Baker Highway (SR 542) to Maple Falls. Turn left on the Silver Lake Rd. It's about 3.5 miles to the park entrance.

## 15. North Cascades National Park Complex

The combined National Park, Ross Lake and Lake Chelan National Recreation Areas comprise one of the largest (3/4 million acres) and most outstanding wilderness recreation areas anywhere in the U.S. Major campgrounds are located at Newhalem, Goodell Creek and Colonial Creek. Fishing and boating are popular on Ross and Diablo Lakes (reservoirs). Hundreds of miles of trails lead up through virgin forests and inspiring meadows, along high scenic ridge tops overlooking glaciers, lakes and clouds. Some of the finest territory is very remote and can only be reached after a day or two backpacking. Still, many day trips are possible. A few are described in this book, while many others can be found in the hiking guides mentioned in the Introduction. Excellent maps and trail information are available through the Marblemount Ranger Station, at Newhalem, and at Sedro Woolley Park headquarters. The Park is east of Marblemount north and south of the North Cascades Highway (SR 20).

# 16. National Wilderness Areas

Three outstanding wilderness areas occupy lands in Whatcom County, including the Mt. Baker and Noisy-Diobsud Wilderness Areas (132,000 acres total) west of the National Park, and the larger Pasayten Wilderness to the east. Major features close to Bellingham include Mt. Baker and the Twin Sisters Range, the Border Peaks, Nooksack Ridge, and numerous lakes, streams, forests, meadows and glaciers surrounding the landmark volcano. The Pasayten extends east of Ross Lake into Okanogan County and contains some of the most remote high country anywhere in the Northwest. Several hundred miles of hiker and horse trails penetrate these wildlands. There are no roads or development in these areas, although camping and boating facilities are available in nearby National Forest and National Recreation Areas. Further information may be obtained from Forest Service Ranger Stations in Sedro Woolley, Mazama and Winthrop.

Efforts to preserve the wilderness qualities of the Mt. Baker region date back to the turn of the century, finally succeeding (partially) in 1984. Spectacular as it is, most of the area is rock and ice, or high elevation old-growth forest not suited to timber harvest (which helps to explain why environmentalists have been so determined to save what little is left of the lower elevation ancient forest). Recreation opportunities are exceptional, to say the least, but in ecological terms, there is still much work to be done to secure a viable future for the wide diversity of plants and animals that call the North Cascades home.

# Viewpoints

## 1. Pt. Roberts Peninsula (Pt. Roberts)

At the county park, there are good views of Canada's Gulf Islands across Georgia Strait. Many birds and occasionally orca and grey whales are seen. Take binoculars. (See walk #1, Lighthouse Point.)

## 2. Semiahmoo Spit (Blaine)

On a fair day, see Drayton Harbor, Semiahmoo Bay, Mt. Baker, the Olympics, and the city of Whiterock, B. C. (See also walk #2, Semiahmoo Spit.)

## 3. Birch Bay

Although Birch Bay can get a little crowded on warm summer weekends, the extensive beach areas at the state park are well worth visiting on weekdays, or anytime between September and May. Take your binoculars for bird life. (See walk #4, Birch Bay to Cherry Point.)

## 4. Cherry Point

This is one of the few good beaches in the county that are not within a park, so there are generally fewer folks around to share it with. The San Juan and Gulf Islands are visible, as are the terminal facilities of the nearby refinery and aluminum industries. (See walk #4, Birch Bay to Cherry Point.)

## 5. Lake Terrell

A beautiful marshy lake, Lake Terrell is a state game range and is popular with fishermen and pheasant hunters. Photographers, canoeists, and bird watchers equally enjoy its serene character. From I-5 (exit 262), head west through downtown Ferndale and stay on the main road as it curves west out of town, becoming Mt. View Road. In 4 miles, turn right on Lake Terrell Rd. The lake is a half-mile north. Return to Mt. View Rd. and continue west a half-mile, curving right on Rainbow Rd. A good viewpoint is on the right (signed).

## 6. Tennant Lake (Ferndale)

The view tower, interpretive center and boardwalk on the lake shore make this worth more than a visit for the view. (*See walk #25, Tennant Lake & Hovander Homestead.*)

## 7. Lummi Island

Lummi Island is great: scenic, little traffic (good for biking), roads are narrow, and the atmosphere is relaxed. From Bellingham, head 14 miles out Marine Dr. and Lummi Shore Dr. (views of Bellingham and Mt. Baker). Or, from I-5 (exit 260), head west on Slater Rd. 3.7 miles, then south on Haxton Rd. about 6 miles to the Lummi Island ferry dock (crossings every hour). On the island, go right for a 7 mile loop around the north end, with great views but few places to get to the water. View the San Juans from Legoe Pt. at the west end of Legoe Bay Rd. A rocky knoll (Lover's Bluff) to the left (private) has been used by the public for many years. If open, respect the owner's kindness and keep your visit brief.

## 8. Squalicum Harbor (Bellingham)

The harbor is the only area of the downtown waterfront that is reasonably accessible to the public. The marina is suitable for an easy stroll to watch boats motor in and out of port. (*See also walk #9, Squalicum Harbor & Historic Bellingham.*)

## 9. Boulevard Park Tower (Bellingham)

Besides offering a fine view of Bellingham Bay, this tower supports a pedestrian bridge over the railroad mainline into Bellingham. Ships and sailboats litter the bay in fair weather. It's easy to see why the bay is so well protected from big stormy seas. Lummi Island and Lummi Peninsula limit the southwesterly fetch to five miles. Stroll along the pier at the park's south end. Canoes have been rented in summer. From downtown, follow State St. and the Boulevard south about 2 miles to Bayview Dr. Turn right at the park sign and drive down the hill to the parking lot. The tower is hard to miss. (*See also walk #13, South Bay Trail.*)

## 10. Sehome Hill Tower (Bellingham)

Certainly the finest vantage point from which to view the city, this tower is located at the north end of the Sehome Hill Arboretum adjacent to Western Washington University (*See walk #11*). Beyond the cityscape are Bellingham Bay, Georgia Strait, the San Juan and Gulf Islands, Whatcom County's lowlands, B.C.'s Coast Range, and Mt. Baker and the Twin Sisters Range. Sunset is a good time to visit. The park closes at dusk. From Samish Way, follow Bill McDonald Parkway and take the first right past the high school. Follow this narrow paved road 3/4 mile to the parking lot at the top. The short path to the tower is well marked.

## 11. Clark Point (Bellingham)

A pleasant spot near the Edgemoor neighborhood overlooking Bellingham Bay, this viewpoint is worth a visit. A significant portion of this outstanding peninsula was recently protected from urban encroachment when the munificent Clark family gave up development rights to the city to ensure its preservation. Please respect their gift. From the Fairhaven bridge, head southwest 1.6 mile on Hawthorn and Fieldston Roads to a Bellingham Parks and Recreation open space sign where the road becomes private. Look for a path on the right and follow it 200 yards to the wooded viewpoint above the railroad tracks. An easy trail to the north leads down toward the water and tracks near a dangerous narrow tunnel. Absolutely do not enter the tunnel: you can't see or hear a train coming from either direction until it's too late. On the east side of the peninsula, a short beach walk is possible at low tide by walking down a wide new trail and a stairway. Cross the tracks and walk the flats as far as a half-mile along the north end of Chuckanut Bay.

## 12. Cyrus Gates Overlook

From the end of the Cleator Rd. (gravel) at Larrabee Park, the view of the San Juan Islands, Samish Bay, Bellingham, western Whatcom County and even Canada is exceptional. Drive 4 miles south of Fairhaven on Chuckanut Drive (SR 11) turning left on the Highline Road just before the park. A sign here also calls this the Cleator Road. The overlook is 3.2 miles away. Scamper up the hill for a view to the east. At the last road switchback (a hard right curve), a good viewpoint of Lost Lake and Mt. Baker is less than a 100 yards distant along an obvious path. (*See also hike #19, Chuckanut Ridge.*)

## 13. Chuckanut Drive

This winding narrow highway (SR 11) is a popular ten mile scenic drive overlooking Bellingham, Chuckanut and Samish Bays. There are numerous turnouts from Larrabee State Park and beyond. Follow the signs south from Fairhaven. Watch out for bicycles, falling rocks and wondrous sunsets.

## 14. Wickersham/Twin Sisters Range

A popular stopping point for travelers on State Highway 9 offers the closest view of the Twin Sisters Range from a paved road. Head north from Wickersham to a highway turnout just north of MP 68. The rural ambiance of the broad South Fork Valley is capped by Mt. Baker just left of the North Twin Sister. The South Twin is flanked on the right by Skookum, Hayden, Little Sister and Cinderella Peaks. A better view of the entire range and the South Fork Valley is from a logging road a mile to the north. Follow it 1.4 miles, stay right, then left in another 0.4 mile. The view is from a large clearcut another mile up this spur. Turn around at the first sharp bend in the clearcut. Caution: this is an active logging area and roads are steep, narrow and may be busy with large trucks. Sundays are normally less truckish and thus a safer time to visit.

## 15. Middle Fork Nooksack Gorge

A nice view of an interesting gorge on the Middle Fork Nooksack River can be reached by way of a 30-minute round trip hike to the City's diversion dam. Water is scooped into a large tunnel blasted through the mountain which empties it into Mirror Lake which in turn drains it to Lake Whatcom. Drive Mt. Baker Hwy to MP 16.8 and go right on Mosquito Lake Rd. In 4.6 miles, go left on Porter Creek Rd. (#38) and park in two-plus miles at a gated spur road next to a sign suggesting we take care of our watershed. Walk the spur to a bridge for the view. Someday a spectacular trail could happen from here to Mosquito Lake Road.

## 16. Mt. Baker Viewpoints

From Bellingham, this great 10,778-foot volcano is mostly obscured by foothills. Often only the top two to three thousand feet are visible, making it appear much smaller and more distant than it actually is (25 miles). The illusion is broken by viewing the peak from a few miles north of Bellingham. Try Noon Road north of Hemmi Road where pastoral farms might interest photographers. Several vantage points exist along the Mt. Baker Highway (SR 542), near Deming and between Maple Falls and Glacier. Try the roadside attraction at MP 29.4 where an informative sign discloses that Captain Vancouver's Lieutenant Baker spotted the mountain in the spring of 1792. Absolutely the best view anywhere by car is at the end of the Glacier Creek Rd. #39. Turn right off Mt. Baker Highway (MP 34.4) just beyond the old ranger station. Mt. Baker and the Black Buttes (an ancient eroded volcanic cone) are visible at several points, but the best view is at the end of the road at 4200 feet, 9.3 miles from the highway. The massive Roosevelt and Coleman Glaciers illustrate why this is considered the iciest of the Cascade volcanoes. Rock features include the "Cockscomb" on the left skyline and the "Roman Nose", an S-shaped ridge extending up the right side of the volcano. Climbers and their tracks can often be seen beneath the Black Buttes (Colfax and Lincoln Peaks) leading to the saddle on the right skyline.

A good view from the southeast is near Baker Lake Dam, a mile east of Baker Lake Rd, about 13 miles north of Highway 20. The Easton, Squak, Talum, Boulder and Park Glaciers appear as one solid mass of ice. In some years, mud flows (lahar) are visible on Boulder Glacier below the steaming crater. (*See hike #47, Morovits Meadows & Park Butte to access Easton Glacier, and viewpoint #17, Artist Point for a good view of the Mazama, Rainbow and Park Glaciers.*)

## 16. Nooksack Falls

One of the largest and most impressive waterfalls in the county is on the North Fork Nooksack River about 7 miles east of Glacier. The viewpoint is perched on a high cliff where the thundering 170-foot falls disappear into mist, tempting a few show-offs to scramble around the fence—DON'T. Because of the contour of the rock walls, the view is not any better anywhere else. (Several have died here recently.) Across the gorge, Wells Creek rushes headlong into the river. Turn right off the Mt. Baker Highway at MP 40.6 on the Wells Creek Rd. #33. Park in a half-mile before the river bridge. On a clear day continue up this road about 5 miles for a good view of Mt. Baker and the Mazama Glacier (*see hike #33, Cougar Divide*).

## 17. Artist Point (July-October)

Drive Mt. Baker Hwy 2.5 miles past the ski area to a parking lot at the road end (may be snowbound into July). Wander the easy trail atop Kulshan Ridge to Huntoon (Artist) Point a half-mile to the southeast. The 360-degree view from Mt. Baker to Mt. Shuksan is incomparable. The Rainbow and Park Glaciers of Mt. Baker gleam in the morning sun, while towering Mt. Shuksan and the ice cliffs of the Curtis and Hanging Glaciers loom to the east. Northward are Tomyhoi, the Border Peaks, Mt. Larrabee and Goat Mt. Baker Lake glistens far below while Glacier Peak and Mt. Rainier glow against a distant smoggy sky. Several other trailheads are located nearby (*see hikes #38, 39, 40 and 41*).

## 18. Picture Lake (year-round)

Follow Mt. Baker Highway to an aptly named Picture Lake at MP 54, just before the ski area. Park at the west end. This view of Mt. Shuksan reflected in the water is said to be the most photographed scene in the North Cascades and the picture is hung on walls around the world. Lighting is best during the later part of the day. The Picture Lake loop trail is an easy subalpine garden walk on a paved path suitable for wheelchairs. The road is plowed to the ski area in winter when the views are even better.

## 19. Goodell Creek

On the way across the North Cascades Highway, a rare glimpse of the towering pinnacles of the southern Picket Range is found at the turnoff to Goodell Creek Campground.

The view is limited and there are no roads or maintained trails into the area. Some of the most challenging alpine mountaineering ascents anywhere in the Cascades are done in this remote region. Turn right off Highway 20 at MP 119.4 and immediately look to the north. Pinnacle Peak, also called the "Chopping Block," is most prominent.

## 20. Gorge Creek Overlook

Beyond Newhalem, the North Cascades Highway enters the spectacular gorge of the Skagit River. A dramatic tributary, Gorge Creek, offers the first good place to get off the road for a few photographs. The signed parking lot is at MP 123.5. Test your fear of heights on a pedestrian catwalk over the gorge, gazing through your feet to the noisy water below. A sizeable waterfall in an old geologic fault intensifies the scene above. (Hang on to your kids!) The creek is dispensing meltwater from the snowfields high on Davis Peak.

## 21. Diablo Lake Overlook

This is a definite stopping point for anyone traveling across the North Cascades Highway. The geological interpretive exhibits are good: you will know exactly what "Skagit Gneiss" looks like when you leave. The views of Diablo Lake, (a Seattle City Light reservoir on the Skagit River), Jack Mountain, and the Colonial Peaks, including Pyramid, Snowfield and Paul Bunyan's Stump, are impressive. In summer the lake turns brilliant green from rock flour carried by streams from the glaciers above. The large parking area is 1.6 mile beyond Colonial Creek Campground (past MP 131).

## 22. Ross Dam

One cannot drive to the dam itself and it's not easy to see from the road. A relatively short trail leads from the highway down to a good view above the dam and reservoir, or you can keep walking to the dam. The trailhead is at MP 134 on the North Cascades Highway. The scenic walk passes a waterfall and loses a bit of elevation on the way to the viewpoint.

## 23. Washington Pass

Another excellent viewpoint, this one is actually ten miles outside of Whatcom County, but it should not be missed during your trip across the North Cascades Highway. From a high cliff at the crest of the Cascade Range, gaze up at the huge rock pinnacles of Liberty Bell Mt. and Early Winter Spires. With binoculars, climbers are often seen ascending the sheer rock faces during fair weather. To the east Silver Star and the Wine Spires shred the skyline. The turn-off is north from the pass (MP 162.4) and is well signed. Follow the paved access road to a parking lot and restrooms. Two easy paths lead to the viewpoint; the lower one is wheelchair accessible.

## 24. Hart's Pass

Hart's Pass and nearby Slate Peak are the highest points you can drive to in the North Cascades. County residents may find it hard to believe that this is still Whatcom County—115 miles from Pt. Roberts. This is the crest of the Cascade Range and the divide between the Skagit and Columbia River basins. The Pacific Crest Trail passes through the area. (*See hike #60, Hart's Pass to Grasshopper Pass, for details and directions.*)

# Campgrounds

*Note: Some campgrounds are open year-round and most are open at least May through October. But many are not, due to seasonal conditions, closures from flooding or wind damage over the winter, or other factors. Call ahead to be sure. Fees and facilities vary.*

## National Forest (360-856-5700)

1. Douglas Fir, *Mt. Baker Hwy (SR 542) near Glacier*
2. Canyon Creek, *Canyon Creek Rd, Mt. Baker Hwy near Glacier*
3. Silver Fir, *Mt. Baker Hwy east of Glacier*
4. Shannon Creek, *Baker Lake Rd off Hwy 20 north of Concrete*
5. Baker Lake, *Baker Lake Rd*
6. Park Creek, *Baker Lake Rd*
7. Boulder Creek, *Baker Lake Rd*
8. Panorama Point, *Baker Lake Rd*
9. Maple Grove, *Baker Lake Rd*
10. Horseshoe Cove, *Baker Lake Rd*

## North Cascades National Park (360-856-5700)

11. Goodell Creek, *N. Cascades Hwy near Newhalem*
12. Newhalem, *North Cascades Hwy at Newhalem*
13. Colonial Creek, *North Cascades Hwy at Diablo Lake*
14. Hozomeen, Ross Lake, *access from Hope, B.C.*

*Ross Lake area campgrounds (trail or boat access only):*

15. Cougar Island
16. Little Beaver
17. Big Beaver
18. Roland Point
19. Rainbow Point
20. Tenmile Island
21. Lightning Creek
22. Cat Island

## Washington State (360-753-2027)

23. Birch Bay State Park, *Birch Bay Dr. south of Blaine*
24. Larrabee State Park, *Chuckanut Dr. (SR 11) south of Bellingham*
25. Hutchinson Creek, *Mosquito Lake Rd near Acme*
26. Rockport State Park, *North Cascades Hwy near Rockport*
27. Cascade Island, *Cascade River Rd near Marblemount*

## Whatcom County (360-733-2900)

28. Lighthouse Marine Park, *Marine Dr. at Pt. Roberts*
29. Bay Horizon Park (hostel), *Alderson Rd near Birch Bay*
30. Silver Lake Park, *Silver Lake Rd, north of Maple Falls*

# Organizations

## Clubs, Etc.

Bellingham Mountaineers, P. O. Box 3187, Bellingham  98227

Bellingham Mountain Rescue Council, P.O. Box 292, Bellingham  98227

Mt. Baker Hiking Club, P.O. Box 73, Bellingham  98227

North Cascades Audubon Society, P.O. Box 5805, Bellingham  98227

Skagit Alpine Club, P.O. Box 513, Mt. Vernon  98273

Washington Native Plant Society, 647 Hunters Pt. Drive, Bellingham  98225

## Agencies

Bellingham Parks & Rec., 3424 Meridian, Bellingham  98225  (360) 676-6985

Glacier Public Service Ctr., Mt. Baker Hwy, Glacier  98244  (360) 599-2714

North Cascades National Park, Sedro Woolley 98284  (360) 856-5700

Marblemount Ranger Station, Marblemount  98267  (360) 873-4590

U. S. Forest Service, Mt. Baker Dist., Sedro Woolley  98284  (360) 856-5700

Wash. DNR, NW Region, Sedro Woolley  98284  (360) 562-6010

Wash. State Parks, 7150 Cleanwater Lane, Olympia  98504  (360) 562-0990

Wash. State Patrol, Bellingham  98225  (360) 676-2076

What. Co. Parks, 3373 Mt. Baker Hwy, Bellingham 98226  (360) 733-2900

What. Co. Sheriff, Courthouse, Bellingham  98225  (360) 676-6650

ALL EMERGENCIES:  CALL 911

# Index

# Hiker's Log

| DATE | TRAIL | MILES | NOTES |
|------|-------|-------|-------|
|      |       |       |       |
|      |       |       |       |
|      |       |       |       |
|      |       |       |       |
|      |       |       |       |
|      |       |       |       |
|      |       |       |       |
|      |       |       |       |
|      |       |       |       |
|      |       |       |       |
|      |       |       |       |
|      |       |       |       |
|      |       |       |       |
|      |       |       |       |
|      |       |       |       |
|      |       |       |       |
|      |       |       |       |
|      |       |       |       |

# Hiker's Log

| DATE | TRAIL | MILES | NOTES |
|------|-------|-------|-------|
|      |       |       |       |
|      |       |       |       |
|      |       |       |       |
|      |       |       |       |
|      |       |       |       |
|      |       |       |       |
|      |       |       |       |
|      |       |       |       |
|      |       |       |       |
|      |       |       |       |
|      |       |       |       |
|      |       |       |       |
|      |       |       |       |
|      |       |       |       |
|      |       |       |       |
|      |       |       |       |
|      |       |       |       |

# Hiker's Log

| DATE | TRAIL | MILES | NOTES |
|------|-------|-------|-------|
|      |       |       |       |
|      |       |       |       |
|      |       |       |       |
|      |       |       |       |
|      |       |       |       |
|      |       |       |       |
|      |       |       |       |
|      |       |       |       |
|      |       |       |       |
|      |       |       |       |
|      |       |       |       |
|      |       |       |       |
|      |       |       |       |
|      |       |       |       |
|      |       |       |       |
|      |       |       |       |
|      |       |       |       |

# Hiker's Log

| DATE | TRAIL | MILES | NOTES |
|------|-------|-------|-------|
|      |       |       |       |
|      |       |       |       |
|      |       |       |       |
|      |       |       |       |
|      |       |       |       |
|      |       |       |       |
|      |       |       |       |
|      |       |       |       |
|      |       |       |       |
|      |       |       |       |
|      |       |       |       |
|      |       |       |       |
|      |       |       |       |
|      |       |       |       |
|      |       |       |       |
|      |       |       |       |